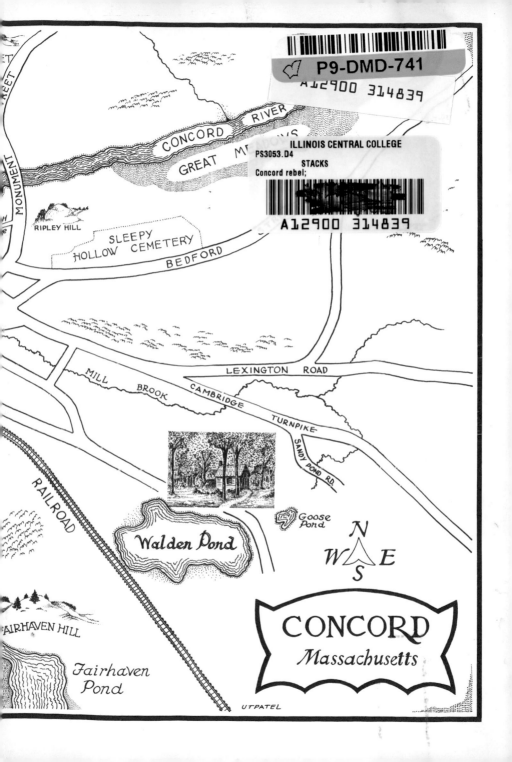

CONCORD RIVER

GREAT MEADOWS

STREET

MONUMENT

RIPLEY HILL

SLEEPY HOLLOW CEMETERY

BEDFORD

MILL BROOK

LEXINGTON ROAD

CAMBRIDGE TURNPIKE

SANDY POND RD.

RAILROAD

Walden Pond

Goose Pond

N
W E
S

FAIRHAVEN HILL

Fairhaven Pond

CONCORD
Massachusetts

UTPATEL

Illinois Central College
Learning Resource Center

CONCORD REBEL

Other Books by AUGUST DERLETH

Walden West
Village Year
Village Daybook
The Wisconsin: River of a Thousand Isles
Still Small Voice: The Biography of Zona Gale
H. P. L.: A Memoir
The Milwaukee Road: Its First 100 Years

Wisconsin in Their Bones
Country Growth
Sac Prairie People
Place of Hawks

Bright Journey
The House on the Mound
The Hills Stand Watch
Wind Over Wisconsin
Restless Is the River
Shadow of Night
Still Is the Summer Night
Evening in Spring
The Shield of the Valiant

Hawk on the Wind
And You, Thoreau!
Rendezvous in a Landscape
Selected Poems
Country Poems
West of Morning

And, for Younger Readers

> The Moon Tenders
> The Mill Creek Irregulars
> The Pinkertons Ride Again
> A Boy's Way
> The Ghost of Black Hawk Island
> Sweet Land of Michigan
> The Country of the Hawk
> The Captive Island
> It's a Boy's World
> Land of Gray Gold
> Land of Sky-Blue Waters
> Fr. Marquette and the Great Rivers
> St. Ignatius and the Company of Jesus
> Columbus and the New World
> Oliver, the Wayward Owl
> Wilbur, the Trusting Whippoorwill

CONCORD REBEL

A LIFE OF
HENRY DAVID THOREAU

By AUGUST DERLETH

CHILTON BOOK COMPANY

PHILADELPHIA   NEW YORK   LONDON

For

WALTER HARDING

who has earned the gratitude of Thoreauvians
throughout the world . . .

Foreword

The single business of Henry Thoreau, during forty-odd years of eager activity, was to discover an economy calculated to provide a satisfying life.
VERNON L. PARRINGTON
Main Currents in American Thought

IT is seldom in the history of mankind that a writer, generally ignored in his lifetime—one whose work has been dismissed by critics and largely gone unread by the public in his own time—should achieve many years after his death an eminent place among the leading writers of his country and among the most influential writers in the world.

Henry David Thoreau was such a writer.

Yet Thoreau was a rebel against the commonly held social credos of his time, a profoundly religious man who had "signed off," as he put it, from his church, a rigid disciplinarian and believer in order who had denied the authority of the state, a poet whose preferred medium of expression was prose, an exponent of freedom of thought in a society which followed the contemporary patterns in popular thought—and valued what Thoreau scorned—material success.

His work is the testament of his rebellion, from *Walden,* which has become the companion of thousands, to *Civil Disobedience,* which was the inspiration of Mahatma Gandhi and other liberal leaders throughout the world.

ix

His life was not one of physical action, but of adventure in the domain of his mind. He found his "occasions" in himself, as he said, and in so doing he achieved the distinction of being "the only man of leisure" in Concord, Massachusetts, because the work he did was less visible to his fellow-citizens than the labor of a ditch-digger. Writing was his "business," he said, and he walked abroad in the environs of his native place "to see what I have caught in my traps, which I set for facts."

Thoreau's vision is one which ought to make an irresistible appeal to the young. No mentally alive young man or woman can read *Walden* and come away from it willing to accept readily the common conventions of the world or the shabby goals set for the mass of men by their materialistic society. "The cost of a thing is the amount of what I call life which is required to be exchanged for it," he wrote, and he went his way through life determined to exact the most from every moment at the least cost in living, and this, despite his limitations—for he was a bachelor, and he made his sacrifices only for himself, which is considerably easier than making sacrifices which might involve dependents in deprivations—he did.

GRATEFUL acknowledgment is made to Houghton Mifflin Company, as the authorized publishers of the works of Henry D. Thoreau, for permission to quote at will from *The Writings of Henry D. Thoreau;* and to the New York University Press, for permission to do likewise from *The Correspondence of Henry D. Thoreau,* edited by Walter Harding and Carl Bode, as well as to the owners of previously unpublished letters appearing for the first time in that book.

Contents

CONCORD REBEL

CHAPTER 1

"If I Knew How It Began . . ."

I came into this world, not chiefly to make this a good place to live in, but to live in it, be it good or bad. —WALDEN

THERE was little in Henry David Thoreau's background and youth to foretell his course in life. He was born July 12, 1817, at his Grandmother Minott's farm on the old Virginia road not far outside Concord, of French-Huguenot and Scottish-Quaker ancestry. When he was baptized three months later by Dr. Ezra Ripley, the leading divine of Concord, he was named David Henry Thoreau, and so he was called until he chose to reverse his given names when he was twenty, at about the time he was graduated from Harvard.

His father was John Thoreau, born in 1787 in Boston. His mother was Cynthia Dunbar, born in the same year in Keene, New Hampshire, the daughter of the Reverend Asa Dunbar. Henry had an older sister, Helen, an older brother, John, and was yet to have a younger sister, Sophia. His father, following the family tradition, had learned storekeeping in Salem and Concord before going into business on borrowed money. He had failed in business, and at the time of Henry's birth the family was quite poor even by the standards of 1817.

Thoreau's earliest years were unsettled because of his father's attempts to establish himself. His father tried his hand at various enterprises. For a while he farmed for

1

his mother-in-law, but he was ill-suited to farming. He next tried keeping a store at Chelmsford, but he failed at this, too, and he turned to keeping a school in Boston, but he had little talent for teaching. He then tried to become a salesman, directing his attention to the Indians who were still to be found in various places throughout New England. This proved so unrewarding that finally, in 1823, when Henry was six, he moved back to Concord and set himself up as a pencil-maker, at which he presently made a modest success.

The Thoreaus were a closely-knit family of lifelong duration. John was a relatively grave man who said very little. He stood somewhat shorter than his wife, and had a tendency toward deafness. He was not prepossessing, but likable, and was far more studious than his wife. Mrs. Thoreau was lively and bustling, with an inclination toward gayety. She was a kindly, shrewd woman, who could sometimes make sharp observations about her fellow-citizens, though she was not in any sense mean and she was very much liked. She loved to talk, and soon had the reputation of being the biggest talker in all Concord. She was also a great reader, much given to sentiment and emotion, and capable of very strong opinions, particularly on such subjects as slavery, to which she was strongly opposed.

Concord was at this time—and remained for most of Thoreau's life—a village of something less than two thousand inhabitants, though the country men who lived in the surrounding township of Concord brought the total population to a little over that figure. It was a typical New England village, one of tree-naved streets lined with white painted houses—as well as some which were not painted at all. There was a village square just past rows of shops put up on a one-time mill dam along a brook. It was a village weighted with ministers at the one end of the social scale, and tavern-keepers at the other. Its most substantial citizens during most of Thoreau's life were Samuel Hoar, the lawyer who owned the most imposing house in the village, and the Reverend Ezra Ripley, pastor of Concord's First Parish, Congregational.

It was a village open to the country on all sides, and the country, so easy of access, was singularly beautiful, not any longer as wild as it had been in the years of Concord's founding over a century and a half before, but still offering the walker in its precincts sight and sound of many a wild creature, furred and feathered. It was a country of little rivers—the Musketaquid or Grassgrown River—the meadow stream, the Sudbury, flowing into the Assabet—which, together, made up the Concord River on its way through marshes and meadows toward the Merrimack. The rivers were bounded by low, glaciated hills, among which were lakes and swamps—one of them, on the way to Cambridge, a pleasant, tree-girt lake named Walden, which charmed Thoreau even as a child. It was a country of pine and hardwood trees, of maple and spruce swamps, of huckleberry and cranberry stands, of knolls like Fair Haven, from which the eye fell upon Wachusett, a small mountain standing solitary in the landscape, and Monadnock.

Except for isolated journeys and his Harvard years, Thoreau's life was bounded by Concord village and town, by Walden and Fair Haven and the rivers. In this setting he spent a boyhood like most boyhoods in New England villages. He drove the cow to pasture, ran barefooted, went fishing—sometimes of nights beside a blazing bonfire to attract the bullheads in Walden Pond—hunted a little, though he abandoned this relatively early in life, and flourished in the aura of his affectionate family. He

3

could hardly help, as a boy, being somewhat dominated by women, for not only was his mother clearly the dominant force in the Thoreau household, but the regular boarders which the Thoreaus took in were all women, not the least among them being Aunt Louisa Dunbar, who joined the household when Grandmother Minott died.

Despite a good sense of humor and easy gregariousness, Thoreau was a grave boy. His gravity earned him the nickname of "Judge," bestowed upon him by no less a local eminence than Samuel Hoar. He soon grew interested in books and learning. He began to go to school in Boston, but he subsequently attended Concord grammar school. He wrote his first essay, *The Seasons,* at the age of ten; it offered no startling clue to what he was to do later in life and demonstrated only that he had a well organized mind, a love of nature, and an ability to write, none of which was unusual among alert children. He had already developed a boy's affection for the countryside and an inclination toward solitude though this was not an indication of the pursuits of his maturity, however much it may seem to have presaged his later life. In his mature years, he referred to his early years in glowing terms, writing in his *Journal,* "My life was ecstasy."

Following grammar school, Thoreau prepared for Harvard at the Concord Academy, which offered courses in Latin, Greek, and French, and where he could learn music and dancing as well. Either here—or from his lively Uncle Charles Dunbar, who led a roving, carefree existence, and of whom Thoreau was very fond—he first learned to play the flute, which was ever afterward to remain part of his life. Certainly here he learned to dance, which was hardly necessary for entry to Harvard.

4

He was ready for Harvard at sixteen. There was scarcely enough money at home to send Thoreau there, though his father could help pay his expenses. By this time Thoreau's sister Helen had begun to teach, and offered to help; so did his aunts. With this support, and sharing the beneficiary funds offered by Harvard to worthy and needy students, Thoreau went to Cambridge in August, 1833, and was entered at Harvard on September 1.

He roomed at Hollis Hall throughout his Harvard years, sometimes alone, sometimes with a roommate. His meals at commons cost him $1.35 a week. Having not yet "signed off" from his church, he attended chapel; he did not wear the required black, but went in a green homespun coat because he did not own and could not afford a black one.

He studied the classics under Professor Felton and Jones Very, a poet who also tutored him. He took rhetoric under Professor Edward Tyrrell Channing, from whose exacting requirements it took Thoreau some time to escape. He was primarily interested in the classics, mastering Greek and Latin early, though he also studied mathematics and, by means of books from the Harvard library, science. Since he knew French, he may also have studied this language at Harvard, and he took an informal course in German at which Henry Wadsworth Longfellow talked about German literature with an informality which, combined with Longfellow's wine-colored waistcoats, very probably left Thoreau cold.

He stood close to the top of his class, but he went his own way too much to reach the top. He made few friends, though there were brief friendships—A. G. Peabody, Henry Vose, Charles Wyatt Rice—evidence of which exists in letters, but none of these was a lasting friendship. One

5

of his classmates, John Weiss, remembered Thoreau at Harvard in a reminiscence-review published in *The Christian Examiner,* July, 1865.

"He would smile to overhear that word (career) applied to the reserve and unaptness of his college life. He was not signalized by a plentiful distribution of the parts and honors which fall to the successful student. . . . We could sympathize with his tranquil indifference to college honors, but we did not suspect the fine genius that was developing under that impassive demeanor. Of his private tastes there is little of consequence to recall, excepting that he was devoted to the old English literature, and had a good many volumes of the poetry from Gower and Chaucer down through the era of Elizabeth. . . .

"But he passed for nothing, it is suspected, with most of us; for he was cold and unimpressible. The touch of his hand was moist and indifferent, as if he had taken up something when he saw your hand coming, and caught your grasp upon it. How the prominent, gray-blue eyes seemed to rove down the path, just in advance of his feet, as his grave Indian stride carried him down to University Hall! This down-looking habit was Chaucer's also, who walked as if a great deal of surmising went on between the earth and him . . .

"He did not care for people; his classmates seemed very remote. This reverie hung always about him, and not so loosely as the odd garments which the pious household care furnished. Thought had not yet awakened his countenance; it was serene, but rather dull, rather plodding. The lips were not yet firm; there was almost a look of smug satisfaction lurking round their corners. . . . The nose was prominent, but its curve fell forward without firmness over the upper lip . . . Yet his eyes were sometimes searching, as if he had dropped, or ex-

6

pected to find, something. It was the look of Nature's own child learning to detect her wayside secrets. . . .

"Thoreau was always indisposed to call at the ordinary places for his spiritual refreshment; and he went farther than most persons when apparently he did not go so far . . .

"But he had no animal spirits for our sport or mischief."

Thoreau was not at home at Harvard as he was in Concord, nor did he make much effort to be. He had come to study. He showed no interest in any of the literary groups or social sets which then flourished at Harvard. He did not contribute to the *Harvardiana*. He appeared to prefer—if not outright solitude—at least obscurity, though he happily accepted the friendship of Charles Stearns Wheeler, one of the promising scholars at Harvard, and went camping with him. Yet he was not lonely, however much alone he was.

He was happy with the library. He read Virgil, Cicero, *The Greek Reader, Adam's Latin Grammar,* Horace, Demosthenes, *Roman Antiquities, Greek Exercises,* Seneca, Euripides, Homer—he read, in fact, all the classics he could get his hands on. To some extent, that reading— and the rhetoric he was taught—was reflected in the themes he wrote for his Harvard classes. Of more than fifty, he saved thirty essays; they were on such topics as *Punishment, The Morality of Lying, The Simple Style, The Superior and the Common Man,* and, curiously, *Shall We Keep Journals?* Yet in his last year at Harvard, he indicated the direction of his thoughts when he wrote in *Conformity in Things Unessential* that duty consisted "in conformity to the dictates of an inward arbiter. . . . Mere conformity to another's habits or customs is never, properly speaking, a duty. . . . The fear of displeasing the world ought not in the least to influence my actions."

Thoreau was not in unbroken attendance during his four years at Harvard. It was the custom of Harvard to allow needy students one leave of absence to earn money. In December, 1835, Thoreau took his leave. He was then 18, and he planned to earn money by teaching. He taught in Canton, Massachusetts, for a period of six weeks, and at Canton stayed with the Reverend Orestes A. Brownson. Brownson was not quite twice Thoreau's age. His own children were in the Canton school, and it was Brownson who examined Thoreau for the position and who recommended him to the board of education.

Brownson was an extraordinarily vital man, hardly the ideal model of a country minister. His mind was ever searching; he was seldom contented with any situation, and he was turning more and more toward the socialist ideal, with a kind of infectious enthusiasm. He was hungry for any new idea and had an idealistic notion of helping labor in his support of the Workingmen's Party. He had only recently gone into the ministry in the Unitarian church, then a great force for intellectual growth within a socio-moral frame. It was perhaps inevitable that something of his enthusiasm would rub off on to Thoreau.

At the time of their introduction to each other, Brownson was studying German. Thoreau joined him in this— perhaps not alone because Brownson was doing it, but because Carlyle, in whose writings Thoreau had developed a strong interest, had done so. In the course of this study Thoreau listened to a flow of ideas the like of which he had not encountered at Harvard. Brownson was Thoreau's first stimulating encounter outside Harvard, and though Thoreau was actually a teacher in the

8

Canton school but a month and a half, yet he was to write to Brownson almost two years later,

"I have never ceased to look back with interest, not to say satisfaction, upon the short six weeks which I passed with you. They were an era in my life—the morning of a new *Lebenstag*. They are to me as a dream that is dreamt, but which returns from time to time in all its original freshness. Such a one as I would dream a second and a third time, and then tell before breakfast."

In the spring of 1836, Thoreau was at home. He may have been ill. He was not teaching. And he was not ill enough to be prevented from accompanying his father to New York to peddle pencils. Tuberculosis was the family illness—as it was that of many families—and Thoreau may have been afflicted with it early in life. Thoreau's absences from Harvard probably did not trouble him overmuch; he was scarcely at ease there as he was in Concord, and his ability to keep up his grades was not in doubt.

Harvard may have made Thoreau scholarly—the point is moot, but his years at Harvard certainly opened to him a world of books to which he had no access in Concord. Other than the Greek and Latin classics, he had read Thomas Carlyle, particularly *Sartor Resartus,* and Carlyle had impressed his youthful mind. He was to write of him later that in his work Carlyle made "the world seem richer for us, the age more respectable, and life better worth the living . . ."

Perhaps more than any other contemporary work, Ralph Waldo Emerson's *Nature* influenced Thoreau. *Nature* was published in 1836; two years earlier Emerson and his family had taken up residence in Concord, and was thereafter to draw to that village many intellectuals. *Nature* was a relatively brief book, but its impact on young readers in the 1830's was tremendous. Thoreau was ready for it. The very first lines of *Nature* must have appealed to him instantly. "To go into solitude, a man needs to retire as much from his chamber as from society. I am not solitary whilst I read and write, though nobody is with me. But if a man would be alone, let him look at the stars." And, a few paragraphs further along, "The lover of nature is he whose inward and outward senses are still truly adjusted to each other." And, still farther along, "We are taught by great actions that the universe is the property of every individual in it."

The man who could write ten years after his graduation from Harvard, in response to an inquiry for a class record, "Though bodily I have been a member of Harvard University, heart and soul I have been far away among the scenes of my boyhood. Those hours that should have been devoted to study, have been spent in scouring the woods and exploring the lakes and streams of my native village."—the pursuits of that boyhood—was clearly ready for Emerson's philosophy.

There is a time in every man's life that is the right time for enlightenment, for exposure to the life of the mind. For Thoreau that time coincided with his reading of *Nature*, though perhaps he was not yet sufficiently impressed by Emerson's, "Each particle is a microcosm, and faithfully renders the likeness of the world," to implement it by deciding then and there to return to Concord and remain there. This came later, though by only two or three years.

But it is not too much to suppose that his quest for truth and his drive toward simplicity began with *Nature*. "A man's power to connect his thought with its proper symbol, and so to utter it, depends on the simplicity of his character, that is, upon his love of truth and his desire to communicate it without loss. . . . All the uses of nature admit of being summed in one, which yields the activity of man an infinite scope. . . . The best read naturalist who lends an entire and devout attention to truth, will see that there remains much to learn of his relation to the world, and that it is not to be learned by any addition or subtraction or other comparison of known quantities, but is arrived at by untaught sallies of the spirit, by a continual self-recovery, and by entire humility." The entire course of Thoreau's life thereafter is evidence that these words of Emerson either profoundly impressed him with a new direction in life, or, what is far more likely, reinforced a bent already firmly rooted.

Life for Thoreau meant living in the environment of his boyhood. He left letters to attest to his friendship with a few classmates—he wrote to Henry Vose in the summer of 1836 urging him to arrange to secure a room for Thoreau ("Your humble servant will endeavor to enter the Senior Class of Harvard University next term, and if you intend taking a room in College, and it should be consistent with your pleasure, will joyfully sign himself your lawful and proper 'Chum.' ")—he wrote to Charles Wyatt Rice urging him to visit ("It would afford me much pleasure if you would visit our good old town this vacation; *in other words, myself.*")—but there is no record to show that Thoreau ever mingled with the students en masse. He never attended his classmates' "evening entertainments" and he ignored his professors' receptions.

Thoreau was ill again for a while during the summer of 1836, for he wrote to Rice that the doctor had forbidden him to indulge in his favorite pastime—which was hunting for Indian remains, in which the Concord area abounded, since Concord had been Indian country before the coming of the white men, and it was possible to find arrowheads and other artifacts anywhere in the vicinity. But "digging and chopping" had been forbidden Thoreau that summer, and perhaps for longer, for Thoreau wrote of his pastime, "the season is past with me."

He was back in college at the end of that summer, and he resumed his more or less restricted way of life—haunting the library, studying, and being relatively reclusive. The tenor of the essays improved; what he had to say in them was more sound and indicated a personal philosophy taking shape, one which owed some debt to Emerson. His essays in this final year of college were more individual and somewhat set apart in content from the typical student's essays he had written earlier.

He was graduated on August 16, 1837. His Commencement address was on *The Commercial Spirit,* in the course of which he said, "This curious world which we inhabit is more wonderful than it is convenient; more beautiful than it is useful; it is more to be admired and enjoyed than used. The order of things should be somewhat reversed; the seventh should be man's day of toil, wherein to earn his living by the sweat of his brow; and the other six his Sabbath of the affections and the soul,— in which to range this widespread garden, and drink in the soft influences and sublime revelations of Nature." —sentiments which come through Thoreau from Emerson's *Nature,* but with Thoreau's own views coloring them.

So he left college. He was not an outstanding student, and he went through his college years leaving not a hint anywhere of what he might become. That his work was satisfactory was attested to some months later when, in response to a request for a recommendation, President Josiah Quincy of Harvard wrote, "I certify that Henry D. Thoreau, of Concord, in this State of Massachusetts, graduated at this seminary in August, 1837; that his rank was high as a scholar in all the branches, and his morals and general conduct unexceptionable and exemplary. He is recommended as well qualified as an instructor, for employment in any public or private school or private family."

CHAPTER 2

First Love

> *If a man does not keep pace with his companions,
> perhaps it is because he hears a different drummer.
> Let him step to the music which he hears, however
> measured or far away. It is not important that he
> should mature as soon as an apple or an oak. Shall
> he turn his spring into summer? If the condition of
> things which we were made for is not yet, what were
> any reality which we can substitute? We will not be
> shipwrecked on a vain reality. Shall we with pains
> erect a heaven of blue glass over ourselves, though
> when it is done we shall be sure to gaze still at the
> true ethereal heaven far above, as if the former
> were not?* —WALDEN

THOREAU returned to Concord. Though he was happy to be back home, he was not yet committed to living in Concord for the rest of his life. He had some thought of teaching. He had been prepared for it, and it seemed to him then the most likely way to make a living. His family found him not quite the same Henry he had been when he left for Harvard in 1833; he was less content to accept opinions as facts, more argumentative, and entirely apt to shock his aunts with his own independent and unconventional opinions.

Secretly, Thoreau wanted to be a poet, but there was no very great drive in him toward that goal. He had no illusions about the economic position of the poet, though a proportionately respectable number of people read

14

poetry in his time. What he wanted most of all was to live as he wished, with freedom to think and act as he pleased; what he had not yet discovered was some kind of economy which would permit this way of life. This was to be his primary concern for the rest of his life.

The only immediate source of income which seemed open to him was teaching. He applied for the public elementary school in Concord and was accepted. In September, scarcely a month after his graduation, he began to teach. He had some vague ideas about education which, by the standards of his day, were decidedly progressive. He let it be known that he would abandon flogging as a punishment, and deliver moral lectures instead. This course hardly impressed the school committee, who were of the opinion that moral lectures did little to enforce discipline.

For two weeks, the committee—and, no doubt, Concord—waited and watched. At the end of that time, one of the committee members visited school and instructed Thoreau to resume the use of the flog and ferule, or the school was likely to suffer in discipline. Thoreau had no intention of being told how to teach. Moreover, he firmly believed that physical punishment should have no part in education. With a fine contempt, he lined up six pupils after school that day, flogged them, and handed in his resignation.

More than all his independent talk, this deed set Thoreau apart. From that moment forward, he was looked upon as queer—which is to say, unconventional to the point of having the wrong values—as people customarily react to everyone whose values differ from their own. He was, in short, a rebel, who showed by his actions that he intended to remain one.

Thoreau went back to pencil-making with his father,

though he had not yet given up the idea of teaching, and made at least one application to a school in Maine. Nothing came of this. Still he cast about; he looked to Virginia, he spoke of going west for a school either alone or with his beloved older brother, John.

Yet the business of making pencils was not onerous. It had grown into a respectable business by this time—though not yet such a business as to place the Thoreau family in the first rank of Concord businessmen. Moreover, it was a happy occupation for a man of Thoreau's temperament; it did not keep him tied down; he kept no regular hours. It was just the sort of occupation which would allow him to do what he liked best—it gave him time for reading, study, and walking about Concord looking for the facts he expected to catch in his "traps."

Thoreau walked the environs of Concord day after day. His favorite walk was to the southwest, which took him through deep woods from Concord toward Sudbury, along the Sudbury River—and south to Fair Haven Hill, Fair Haven Pond, and Walden Pond. It took him past the Hosmer farm, where he liked to stop, for he was already beginning to enjoy the company of people who lived close to the earth over that of the presumably "best" people of Concord. Northeast of Concord lay the Great Meadows and Ball's Hill, along the Concord River, and directly north rose Ponkawtasset. Thoreau had known them all from his earlier years, and he set about now to improve his acquaintance with them.

Late in October of that year, he began his *Journal*. Journals were commonly kept by men and women in that day, and diaries were even more common. Under date of October 22, 1837, Thoreau recorded that someone had asked him, "What are you doing now? Do you keep a journal?"—and added, "So I make my first entry."

It was to be a life's work, though at first it may not have seemed so to Thoreau.

A little later, under the same date, he wrote, "I seek a garret." He preferred living in a garret, and that preference remained with him. The Thoreau family were then living in the Parkman house, and Thoreau lived "upstairs"—in the garret, if there were one to be had. "The spiders must not be disturbed, nor the floor swept, nor the lumber arranged."

On his walks Thoreau carried with him a notebook and pencil, so that he might jot down such thoughts as occurred to him, or those incidents of the life of woods and marshes and rivers that might catch his eye, to be expanded later in the solitude of his garret. He frequently also carried a spy-glass with which to watch birds and animals going about their affairs, and also a *Primo Flauto*—his father's old music book—in which to press plants he gathered as specimens.

He used his journal also very largely to copy lines and paragraphs from the books he was then reading. These were chiefly classical—Ossian, Homer, Donne, Chaucer, Anacreon, Pliny, Aristotle, Virgil, Tasso, Goethe. Generous quotations from these sources vied for place with accounts of his walks—like the story of a walk taken with John in the course of which, by coincidence, after a conversation about Indians and Henry's declaration that "There is Tahatawan's arrowhead," they found an arrowhead on that fanciful spot—and the direction of his thoughts—"My desire is to know *what* I have lived, that I may know *how* to live henceforth." He also set down in his journal the gist of essays he hoped to write later, and, perhaps, publish in the magazines of the day, as well as later, in a book.

Thoreau's journal was no private affair. It was read

by the members of his family, especially his sister Helen, and it was drawn to the attention of one of the ladies who had boarded at the Thoreaus earlier in 1837, Mrs. Lucy Jackson Brown. Mrs. Brown was visiting one autumn afternoon and the two ladies were discussing a recent lecture of Ralph Waldo Emerson's, when Helen said that Henry wrote similarly in his journal. At Mrs. Brown's request, the journal was produced—far be it from Thoreau to keep it under lock and key—and Mrs. Brown read in it. Not surprisingly, some of the notes Thoreau had set down paralleled things Emerson had said or written.

Mrs. Brown happened to be an older sister of Emerson's second wife, Lidian. It was only natural that she should bring to Emerson information that there was in the immediate vicinity a young man whose thoughts echoed Emerson's. Emerson, who was always interested in the young—though he was only fourteen years older than Thoreau—asked that he be brought to the house. Emerson may not have known who Thoreau was at that time, but certainly Thoreau knew all about Emerson, for, as a younger schoolmate of Thoreau's, George Hoar, chronicled in his own autobiography many years later, Thoreau had walked eighteen miles from Concord to Boston—and back by night—solely to hear Emerson lecture.

Emerson was in these years an inspiration to the young. He encouraged them to revolt against outmoded beliefs, to challenge conventions, particularly in thought, to strive toward knowledge of themselves and to express themselves. It was typical of Thoreau that he had made no effort tc call upon Emerson previously; it was like him to pursue his own solitary way without regard for the opinions of the famous, the godly, the wealthy, or the learned neighbors of Concord; but an invitation to visit he did not turn down.

Thoreau left no record of his first meeting with Emerson, the beginning of an important, if not always easy, friendship. Very probably Emerson saw Thoreau, then in his twenty-first year, as a disciple. By early February of 1838—not long after their first meeting—Emerson was writing of Thoreau in his own journal, "I delight much in my young friend, who seems to have as free and erect a mind as any I have ever met."—and, a week later, "My good Henry Thoreau made this else solitary afternoon sunny with his simplicity and clear perception. . . . Everything that boy says makes merry with society, though nothing can be graver than his meaning." It was not improbable that Emerson saw in Thoreau a reflection of himself, ground which had proved fertile for Emerson's ideas.

On another score there was sufficient evidence to persuade Emerson in his lighter moments to fancy that he had invented—or at least prophesied—Thoreau. Three years before, while Thoreau was still a sophomore at Harvard, unknown to Emerson save as a lad from the village, Emerson had written in his journal, "If life were long enough, among my thousand and one works should be a book of nature whereof Howitt's *Seasons* should be not so much the model as the parody. It should contain the natural history of the woods around my shifting camp for every month of the year. It should tie their astronomy, botany, physiology, meteorology, picturesque, and poetry together. No bird, no bug, no bud, should be forgotten on his day and hour." By 1838 Emerson had put aside this dream, but here was young Henry Thoreau traveling widely in Concord and setting down just such a record in his journal.

19

From that initial visit onward, Thoreau was welcome at the Emerson house, and particularly at those evenings of stimulating conversation so much a part of Emerson's life. These evenings could hardly have been described as ordinary. He might meet there Edmund Hosmer, his farmer friend, but he might also meet the versatile and colorful Margaret Fuller or Jones Very, the poet. He saw citizens of Concord next to people like Elizabeth Peabody, a distinguished educator, or Sarah Bradford, a renowned Greek scholar, or Bronson Alcott, the idealistic pioneer in education, who was himself to take up residence in Concord in 1840. Thoreau took part in the stimulating gatherings, but he was not essentially a part of the group which came together at Emerson's. He took what he liked of the ideas which were scattered there like chaff, and rejected the rest, quite as at a table he was wont only to partake of those viands which suited his palate.

The visitors at Emerson's were interested in anything new, particularly new avenues of thought. Freedom of thought was their ideal—it was Thoreau's, too. Many of them called themselves Transcendentalists after a pattern of thinking which took its ideas from life's laws and looked for truth, however idealistically, in consciousness and awareness itself, rather than in sense. Constantly in search of the ideal, always embattled against materialism, the Transcendentalists appealed to Emerson, but the movement—such as it was—never completely involved him, much though he enjoyed listening to the ideas of his guests. He might lend them his prestige now and then, or offer them a protecting wing, but never his mind's independence. Nor did it involve Thoreau. If now and then he called himself a Transcendentalist, he forgot it in a few days. From the ideas of the Transcendentalists he took, too, what suited his nature, and ignored the rest; he took only what seemed to him of help in his struggle to come to terms with life in Concord.

Undeniably, these evenings stimulated him. He was a member of the Concord Lyceum, where audiences listened to lectures by local luminaries as well as by hired speakers. On April 11, 1838, Thoreau delivered his first lecture on *Society*. It was not such a lecture as to set minds afire, but rather more rhetoric and pedanticism, but now and then there were glimpses of the later Thoreau. He said, for example, that some of his fellow citizens were "newly shingled and clapboarded," but a knock brought no answer for there was no one at home. *Society* was only the first of a series of lectures, though Thoreau performed other services for the Lyceum, not the least of which was the programming in one season, when he retained twenty-five speakers at a total cost of a hundred dollars.

In May of that year he set out by boat from Boston for two weeks in Maine. From Portland he went to Bath and Brunswick. "Each one's world is but a clearing in the forest, so much open and inclosed ground," he wrote in his journal. He went to Augusta by way of Gardiner and Hallowell, and then on to Bangor and to Oldtown, where he encountered an Indian. He was much interested in Indians and hoped some day to write a book about them. "I had much conversation with an old Indian at the latter place (Oldtown), who sat dreaming upon a scow at the waterside and striking his deer-skin moccasins against the planks, while his arms hung listlessly by his side. He was the most communicative man I had met."

By May 17 he was back in Boston and once more on

21

his rounds. He had put in an apprenticeship in poetry, and his journal contains many of the poems he wrote celebrating a variety of things—*May Morning, Cliffs,* truth, goodness, beauty, *My Boots, Friendship, The Bluebirds, Walden*—

>. . . Only the practiced ear can catch the surging words
>That break and die upon thy pebbled lips.
>Thy flow of thought is noiseless as the lapse
>   of thy own waters . . .

and *Fair Haven*—

>When winter fringes every bough
>With his fantastic wreath,
>And puts the seal of silence now
>Upon the leaves beneath;
>
>When every stream in its penthouse
>Goes gurgling on its way,
>And in his gallery the mouse
>Nibbleth the meadow hay;
>
>Methinks the summer still is nigh,
>And lurketh there below,
>As that same meadow mouse doth lie
>Snug underneath the snow. . . .

Meanwhile, there was still the problem of making a living other than in manufacturing and selling pencils. Teaching continued to seem to Thoreau the only course open to his limited talents. In June, 1838, he established himself as master of a private school held in the Parkman house. His reputation as an eccentric had not injured his standing as a teacher, for he had enough pupils to keep him occupied. Presumably the school made progress, for in three months both he and his brother John were teaching in the newly reopened Concord Academy.

The Academy soon had a waiting list. There was a widespread distrust of public schools among the leading citizens of the region. Boys came not only from Concord but from beyond. Some of the boys boarded with the Thoreau family, so that Henry and John saw them not only in school but out. John was in nominal charge of the school, and was especially popular with small children. Henry taught mathematics and the classical courses, and either he or his brother opened each day with a little talk to preface the lessons of the day.

The Thoreau brothers offered a curriculum that satisfied the educational standards of the day, and more. They took the students out for hikes through the countryside, trips on the river, in search of arrowheads, birding, on flower hunts, in the course of which Henry or John shared their knowledge with the students in their charge. It was a happy school for the children. Small wonder that discipline was no problem; there was no flogging and there were no moral lectures, for lack of need.

Yet the school seems not to have fulfilled Thoreau's expectations financially for, in early October of that year, he wrote to Taunton, Massachusetts, seeking a position in a school there because his "present school . . . is not sufficiently lucrative." Nothing came of this, and the Academy continued with John and Henry Thoreau to serve its students.

Dissatisfied Thoreau might have been, but he could hardly have been unhappy. He fed his soul on his long walks into the country around Concord, and his mind basked in the reflected brilliance of the gatherings at Emerson's or in its own white light. To Emerson, Thoreau was already *"the* man of Concord," which was a salute to the quality of Thoreau's thinking, rather than to his written work, which was to Emerson no more than "good poetry and better prose." He walked frequently with Emerson, discoursing on philosophical matters and on life. Their relationship was that of master and pupil—Thoreau absorbing Emerson's ideas, Emerson delighted to see his ideas fall upon such fertile soil.

The year turned.

In that year of 1839 there were, among the Thoreau boarders, the Wards. Miss Prudence Ward taught drawing and gave some lessons in botany. She wrote at great length about the Thoreau boys to her sister, who was the wife of the Reverend Edmund Sewall in Scituate, and they exchanged frequent visits. In June, young Edmund Sewall came along to visit, and Thoreau found himself so much attracted to this eleven-year-old boy that he wrote a poem, *Sympathy,* to celebrate the boy's "pure, uncompromising spirit," as Thoreau put it in his journal under date of June 22. "Some persons carry about them the air and conviction of virtue . . . when they are near it is like an invisible presence which attends you."

The following month Edmund's sister Ellen came to Concord. She was a beautiful, gay, affectionate girl, and she arrived in midsummer, the time of vacation at the Academy. The Thoreau boys showed her about Concord. Henry squired her up and down the Assabet. Aunt Prudence chaperoned. She was in Concord for three weeks, and both the Thoreau boys fell in love with her, apparently without mutual knowledge.

On the day of her arrival, July 20, Thoreau put into his journal a poem titled *The Breeze's Invitation* which contained such lines as "I the king and you the queen . . . To our music Time will linger . . ." and clearly celebrated her arrival. Five days later he wrote a single, poignant line, "There is no remedy for love but to love more." Thereafter there is no entry in the journal until

24

late August. Undoubtedly Thoreau's thoughts were taken up by Ellen Sewall, and his feelings for her must have given him many troubled hours.

On that last day of August, Ellen Sewall had returned to Scituate, and the Thoreau brothers were embarking on a holiday together, one much to their liking. They were going by boat down the Concord River, and meant to take the Middlesex Canal into the Merrimack River to follow that stream as far as the vicinity of Hooksett, New Hampshire, from which they intended to walk deeper into New Hampshire before returning to Concord.

The trip was an idyll which Thoreau never forgot. Out of it was to come his first book. Undoubtedly he kept copious notes, but what remains in his journal gives little clue to the material which ultimately appeared in that first book. His initial entry sets forth what he saw, the things that his senses apprehended. On that first day the brothers "Made seven miles, and moored our boat on the west side of a little rising ground which in the spring forms an island in the river, the sun going down on one hand, and our eminence contributing its shadow to the night on the other."

Thoreau continues: "In the twilight so elastic is the air that the sky seems to tinkle over farmhouse and wood. Scrambling up the bank of our *terra incognita* we fall on huckleberries, which have slowly ripened here, husbanding the juices which the months have distilled, for our peculiar use this night. If they had been rank poison, the entire simplicity and confidence with which we plucked them would have insured their wholesomeness. The devout attitude of the hour asked a blessing on that repast. It was fit for the setting sun to rest on. . . .

"From our tent here on the hillside, through that isos-

25

celes door, I see our lonely mast on the shore, it may be as an eternity fixture, to be seen in landscapes henceforth, or as the most temporary standstill of time, the boat just come to anchor, and the mast still rocking to find its balance. . . .

"The musquash by the boat is taking toll of potatoes and melons. Is not this the age of a community of goods? His presumption kindles in me a brotherly feeling. Nevertheless, I get up to reconnoitre, and tread stealthily along the shore to make acquaintance with him. But on the riverside I can see only the stars reflected in the water, and now, by some ripple ruffling the disk of a star, I discover him."

By the second night, they had reached Tyngsborough on the Merrimack where they "camped under some oaks . . . on the east bank . . . just below the ferry." By Wednesday they had reached Hooksett, and on the following day, September 5, they "Walked to Concord (New Hampshire), 10 miles." Thereafter for a week they walked—to Franconia Notch "and saw the Old Man of the Mountain," and to other places in that state before riding back to Hooksett and rowing to Bedford "near the ferry, by a large island, near which we camped." After that they rowed and sailed back to their home village.

Each must have been secretly engrossed with thoughts of lovely Ellen Sewall, for they were no sooner back in Concord than John went to visit in Scituate and walked out with Ellen. And in December both the Thoreau boys visited the Sewalls, taking Miss Prudence Ward along with them. Returning, John sent Ellen opals for her collection, and Henry sent her some of the poems he had written.

The winter put an end to visiting, if not to correspondence. By this time Thoreau's interest was being enlisted in the Transcendentalists' newest venture—a magazine. In common with literary groups since the dawn of time, the Transcendentalists were planning to publish a magazine so that they might have a rostrum from which to announce their beliefs, vague as they were, to the world. It was to be called *The Dial,* and Margaret Fuller was to be its editor. Perhaps Thoreau could contribute?

He sent her *Sir Walter Raleigh,* which she rejected. Then he sent her *Aulus Persius Flaccus,* a study of the Latin poet, which she accepted for the first number, which was to be dated July, 1840. Thoreau now intended to try his hand at writing, but he could hardly have had any conviction that a creative career was the answer to his economic problems.

Teaching still remained to him the only answer, and even this was not entirely satisfactory. It may have begun to pall. In spite of it, Thoreau had ample leisure in which "to improve his soul's estate." On March 21, 1840, he recognized his position in the world when he wrote in his journal: "I am freer than any planet; no complaint reaches round the world. I can move away from public opinion, from government, from religion, from education, from society. Shall I be reckoned a ratable poll in the county of Middlesex, or be rated at one spear under the palm trees of Guinea? Shall I raise corn and potatoes in Massachusetts, or figs and olives in Asia Minor? sit out the day in my office in State Street, or ride it out on the steppes of Tartary? For my Brobdingnag I may sail to Patagonia; for my Lilliput, to Lapland. In Arabia and Persia, my day's adventures may surpass the Arabian Nights' Entertainments. I may be a logger on the head waters of the Penobscot, to be recorded in fable hereafter as an amphibious river-god, by as sounding a name as Triton or Proteus; carry furs from Nootka to China, and so be more renowned than Jason and his golden fleece; or go on a South Sea exploring expedition, to be hereafter recounted along with the periplus of Hanno. I may repeat the adventures of Marco Polo or Mandeville.

"These are but few of my chances, and how many more things may I do with which there are none to be compared!" But Thoreau did none of them; he was actively about the exploration of Concord and its environs, and he recognized that "Our limbs, indeed, have room enough, but it is our souls that rust in a corner," knowing that it was not important who one might be or where he might go, but *what* he was that mattered.

His love for Ellen Sewall continued unabated. One might guess that he walked all that winter and spring on lighter feet, waiting upon renewed sight of the visitor from Scituate.

In June she came. No doubt the Thoreau brothers vied for her attention. Henry took her rowing one day, and on June 19 wrote in his journal, "The other day I rowed in my boat a free, even lovely young lady, and, as I plied the oars, she sat in the stern, and there was nothing but she between me and the sky. So might all our lives be picturesque if they were free enough, but mean relations and prejudices intervene to shut out the sky, and we never see a man as simple and distinct as the man-weathercock on a steeple."

Perhaps he was already aware that the elder Sewalls, while accepting the Thoreau boys as acquaintances or friends, had some reservations about their becoming relatives. The Sewalls were conservative Unitarians, and the Thoreaus, by their standards, were radical. Late in July Ellen returned to Scituate, with her Aunt Prudence, her Grandmother Ward, and John Thoreau. While he was there, Ellen later related, John proposed. She accepted his proposal, but the engagement did not last long—less than a month. It was broken amicably, for John and Ellen continued to correspond.

Henry's turn came next. At the end of October he wrote his proposal to Ellen, but he had no great confidence that it would be accepted, and his journal entries for early November offer evidence that he anticipated her rejection.

It came with almost crushing finality. Her father directed her to write to Henry as coldly and briefly as possible in rejection. Though she wrote her Aunt Prudence that she "never felt so badly" at having to do so, she was herself of essentially the same mind. She enjoyed the company of the Thoreau brothers, but she never had any real intention of marrying either one of them.

It is doubtful that Henry had any real longing for the married state, either.

Though he never lost the memory of Ellen Sewall, Thoreau was speedily resigned to her passing out of his life. He dreamed of her, he made references to her in what he wrote, however disguised, and in January he wrote in his journal, "To sigh under the cold, cold moon for a love unrequited is but a slight on nature; the natural remedy would be to fall in love with the moon and the night and find our love requited."

He could now give all his attention to devising some means of making his living by writing.

CHAPTER 3

"A Singular Character"

> *Time is but the stream I go a-fishing in. I drink at it; but while I drink I see the sandy bottom and detect how shallow it is. Its thin current slides away, but eternity remains. I would drink deeper; fish in the sky, whose bottom is pebbly with stars. I cannot count one. I know not the first letter of the alphabet. I have always been regretting that I was not as wise as the day I was born. The intellect is a cleaver; it discerns and rifts its way into the secret of things. I do not wish to be any more busy with my hands than is necessary. My head is hands and feet. I feel all my best faculties concentrated in it. My instinct tells me that my head is an organ for burrowing, as some creatures use their snout and fore paws, and with it I would mine and burrow my way through these hills. I think that the richest vein is somewhere hereabouts; so by the divining-rod and thin vapors I judge; and here I will begin to mine.*
>
> —WALDEN

MORE than ever, Thoreau sought the solitary instruction of the woods and fields, the rivers and hills of the town. He still taught with his brother, but he had not given himself to teaching. Little of those hours in the classroom made its way into the pages of his journal, and increasingly more of the countryside and Thoreau's experience—both physical and mental—was set down.

On the 30th of January, 1841, Thoreau walked to Fair Haven Pond, marking the trails of foxes, and then suddenly saw a fox down river—sixty rods away, heading for the woods. Five inches of snow covered the ground, and the fox, he saw, was experiencing some difficulty. Thoreau decided to chase him and took off with "head aloft . . . snuffing the air like a fox-hound, and spurning the world and the Humane Society at each bound. It seemed the woods rang with the hunter's horn, and Diana and all the satyrs joined in the chase and cheered me on. Olympian and Elean youths were waving palms on the hills."

The fox, however, was Nature's own child, and Thoreau not alone Nature's. The fox doubled and "I wheeled and cut him off, bounding with fresh vigor, Antaeuslike, recovering my strength each time I touched the snow. Having got near enough for a fair view, just as he was slipping into the wood, I gracefully yielded him the palm."

This was Thoreau in his element.

The journal for that year was filled with observations of nature, with aphorisms, and thoughtful passages testifying to Thoreau's growth. "There is always a single ear in the audience, to which we address ourselves," he wrote—and if that ear were his own. "We are constantly invited to be what we are; as to something worthy and noble. I never waited but for myself to come round; none ever detained me, but I lagged or tagged after myself." And, "My life must seem as if it were passing at a higher level than that which I occupy. It must possess a dignity which will not allow me to be familiar." And, "Brave speaking is the most entire and richest sacrifice to the gods,"—like that, perhaps, which made him seem argumentative at some of those gatherings at Emerson's.

He was happy to be a part of Nature. "I feel slightly

complimented when Nature condescends to make use of me without my knowledge, as when I help scatter her seeds in my walk, or carry burs and cockles on my clothes from field to field." Many passages in the journal testify to his delight on his hikes into the country. "My life at this moment is like a summer morning when birds are singing. Yet that is false, for nature's is an idle pleasure in comparison: my hour has a more solid serenity. I have been breaking silence these twenty-three years and have hardly made a rent in it."

He kept his journal with more than one purpose. He was setting down in it notes he hoped to use in work he could publish later in his life. He was improving his prose style, slowly escaping from Professor Channing's rhetoric. He was keeping a literary—rather than a sci-entific—record of Nature in the environs of Concord. In its fourth year, he saw his journal as "that of me which would else spill over and run to waste, gleanings from the field which in action I reap. I must not live for it, but in it for the gods. They are my correspondent, to whom daily I send off this sheet postpaid. I am clerk in their counting-room, and at evening transfer the account from day-book to ledger. . . . It is always a chance scrawl, and commemorates some accident,—as great as earth-quake or eclipse."

Another objective beyond mere hiking and observation was gradually taking shape in Thoreau's mind. He wanted a place of his own—some country retreat not too far from Concord, so that he might still make his regular way along the Mill Dam and take part in the current of village gossip, as always, and be in attendance at Emerson's gatherings, and drop in on his mother and sisters from time to time. He wanted such a place as

32

might still permit him to teach and make pencils, thus doing the things he must do to earn some income while he perfected his writing to a point where it might either supplement his small income or replace it, which he would much have preferred.

He thought about buying the orchard side of Fair Haven Hill, the Baker Farm, the Cliff Hill, and Weird Dell, but he finally fixed upon Hollowell Farm, which served all his requirements. He set down its attractions— "its complete retirement, being at least two miles from the village, half a mile from any neighbor, and separated from the highway by a broad field; its bounding on the river; the pleasing ruin of the house and barn; the hollow and lichen-covered apple trees gnawed by rabbits; above all the recollection I had of it from my earliest voyages up the river, when the house was concealed behind a dense grove of red maples, which then stood between it and the river, through which I once heard the house-dog bark; and in general the slight improvements that swayed, though I did not mention them to the proprietor. To enjoy these things I was ready to carry it on and do all those things which I now see had no other motive or excuse but that I might pay for it and be unmolested in my possession of it; though I knew all the while that it would yield the most abundant crop of the kind I wanted if I could only afford to let it alone. Though it afforded no western prospect, the dilapidated fences were picturesque. I was in some haste to buy, before the proprietor finished getting out some rocks, cutting down some hollow apple trees, and grubbing up some young birches which had sprung up in the pasture, all which in my eyes very much enhanced its value."

He was aware that ownership of such a property en-

33

tailed certain responsibilities, even though those responsibilities might earn him an income. "I must not lose any of my freedom by being a farmer and landholder," he wrote in his journal. "Most who enter on any profession are doomed men. The world might as well sing a dirge over them forthwith. The farmer's muscles are rigid. He can do one thing long, not many well. . . . I can leave this arable and grass ground, without making a will or settling my estate. . . . I would buy a farm as freely as a silken streamer. . . . My life must undulate still."

He was not called upon to make any difficult choice. He had no money with which to buy the Hollowell Farm or any other. He wanted to buy the farm on credit, and, while the owner was willing, his wife was not. This ended his hope of owning the Hollowell Farm, but did not put an end to his aspirations. "I only ask a clean seat," he wrote in his journal on April 5. "I will build my lodge on the southern slope of some hill, and take there the life the gods send me. Will it not be employment enough to accept gratefully all that is yielded me between sun and sun?"

His economic circumstances were not to improve. Indeed, they weakened. Early in 1841 his brother John took sick, very probably with an attack of tuberculosis, the family ailment. He struggled along with the school for a while, but not for long. On April first, the school was closed, and another source of his income was at an end. He very likely saw the end of teaching without regret, for he certainly found it onerous and an interference with his inspection of the countryside around Concord. Nothing of the school's closing appears in the journal, unless a curious poem, *On the Sun Coming Out in the Afternoon—*

34

Methinks all things have travelled since you shined,
But only Time, and clouds, Time's team, have moved;
Again foul weather shall not change my mind,
But in the shade I will believe what in the sun I loved.

may be considered an indirect reference to it.

Thoreau may have wondered what he might do to earn money while he improved his writing, still hoping to make a living by writing, which was scarcely a rational hope in his time, but he made no effort to do anything but the most casual kind of occasional labor. However, his friend Emerson was not unaware of his situation, and was convinced that one so full "of buds of promise" ought to be given a helping hand.

Emerson asked Thoreau whether he would not like to come and take the place of the chore boy he had had. Emerson was frequently away from home, lecturing—sometimes for months—and he wanted someone who might serve as a handyman at the house. He had grown weary, too, of caring for the property. All this Thoreau could do, and none of it would tax him very much. It was the kind of position which fitted Thoreau in that it would still permit him to take his jaunts along the river and into the woods.

Less than four weeks after the school closed, Thoreau moved into an upstairs room at Emerson's. What Thoreau's intimate thoughts about this shift in his fortunes were is not recorded. His journal for the day—April 26, 1841—is laconic in its entry. "Monday. At R. W. E.'s." There follows a paragraph about the charm of the Indian—a lifelong interest of Thoreau's—and one pungent line—"It is a great art to saunter."

He discharged those duties which he had accepted and still had ample time to pursue his favorite occupation. A month later, at May's end, he was at Walden Pond. "I sit in my boat on Walden, playing the flute this evening, and see the perch, which I seem to have charmed, hovering around me, and the moon travelling over the bottom, which is strewn with the wrecks of the forest, and feel that nothing but the wildest imagination can conceive of the manner of life we are living. Nature is a wizard. The Concord nights are stranger than the Arabian nights." His life was perhaps more idyllic than he knew, even though it was understood that, apart from his board and room, there was to be no payment for Thoreau's services.

Emerson meant Thoreau to have the leisure to develop. He wrote to his brother William that if Thoreau could only fall in love, it might "sweeten him and straighten him."

His sojourn at Emerson's enlarged Thoreau's horizons and in a sense also his family. Not only did he have his own closely-knit family to visit, but he had recourse to the pensive Lidian Emerson, Emerson's second wife, and the Emerson children. He was also in more intimate touch with the Transcendentalists and others who regularly called at the Emerson house, but he continued to hold himself a little aloof from them. He took part in their discussions, but a prickly sort of part, on his own terms, unwilling to accept without challenge what the Transcendentalists held to be gospel.

For Mrs. Emerson—and her sister, Mrs. Lucy Jackson Brown, with whom he corresponded—Thoreau had an affection not unlike that he had for his mother and sisters, but an affection uncomplicated by family obligations. He felt that he could open himself to these sisters as to few other women. He could write to Mrs. Brown, "We always seem to be living just on the brink of a pure and lofty intercourse which would make the ills and trivialness of life ridiculous." But at this brink Thoreau was happy to remain. "I am very happy in my present environment," he wrote.

He was more likely to write of himself—"I grow savager and savager every day, as if fed on raw meat"— and indeed, he had begun to eat woodchuck, as indulgence in a new experience, one of which he soon had enough—"and my tameness is only the repose of untamableness. I dream of looking abroad summer and winter, with free gaze, from some mountain-side, while my eyes revolve in an Egyptian slime of health,—I to be nature looking into nature with such easy sympathy as the blue-eyed grass in the meadow looks in the face of the sky. From some such recess I would put forth sublime thoughts daily, as the plant puts forth leaves. Now-a-nights I go on to the hill to see the sun set, as one would go home at evening; the bustle of the village has run on all day, and left me quite in the rear; but I see the sunset, and find that it can wait for my slow virtue."

Living at the Emerson house had one more important advantage—it gave Thoreau access to Emerson's library. There he made the acquaintance of Hindu philosophy in *The Laws of Menu* and, later, in the *Bhagavad-Gita*, which had as profound an influence on him as anything he ever read. He had not been in residence five weeks before he was reading these books. He mentioned *The Laws of Menu* in his journal as early as May 31; by June 7 he wrote, "I know of no book which comes to us with grander pretensions . . . What wonder if the times were not ripe for it?" Thereafter he recorded his enthusiasm frequently—

August 6th, for instance—"I cannot read a sentence in the book of the Hindoos without being elevated as

37

upon the table-land of the Ghauts. It has such a rhythm as the winds of the desert, such a tide as the Ganges, and seems as superior to criticism as the Himmaleh Mounts. Even at this late hour, unworn by time, with a native and inherent dignity it wears the English dress as indifferently as the Sanscrit. The great tone of the book is of such fibre and such severe tension that no time nor accident can relax it."

And the next day, "The impression which those sublime sentences made on me last night has awakened me before any cockcrowing. Their influence lingers around me like a fragrance, or as the fog hangs over the earth late into the day." And later—"Any book of great authority and genius seems to our imagination to permeate and pervade all space. Its spirit, like a more subtle ether, sweeps along with the prevailing winds of the country. Its influence conveys a new gloss to the meadows and the depths of the wood . . . All things confirm it." And later still—"In the Hindoo scripture the idea of man is quite illimitable and sublime. There is nowhere a loftier conception of his destiny. . . . There is no grander conception of creation anywhere. It is peaceful as a dream, and so is the annihilation of the world."

He did not abandon the Greeks for the Hindus, however. He read voraciously, but there is less of the Greeks in his journals for the years he spent at Emerson's house. And nothing he read shook his foundations, but only reinforced them. He continued to write, and some of his verses appeared in 1841 in *The Dial,* which offered an outlet for so many of Emerson's young friends when other markets, more staid, were closed to them.

And he held to the ideal of a place of his own. On Christmas Eve that year he wrote in his journal, "I want to go soon and live away by the pond, where I shall hear

38

only the wind whispering among the reeds. It will be success if I shall have left myself behind. But my friends ask what I will do when I get there. Will it not be employment enough to watch the progress of the seasons?"

Thoreau's idyllic life was, however, to sustain a new and profoundly shaking experience, which was to bring home to him the aloof impartiality of Nature as perhaps nothing else had done to this time. Early in January, 1842, his brother John, while shaving one day, cut himself. The wound healed, but tetanus set in, and on the 12th John died in agony. Thoreau, ever close to his older brother, was deeply affected; he was unable to set down a note in his journal, and his grief was compounded when Emerson's son, Waldo, died of scarlet fever only a fortnight later.

It was five weeks before he made another entry in the journal. "I feel as if years had been crowded into the last month, and yet the regularity of what we call time has been . . . preserved . . ." he wrote on February 21. Three weeks later he wrote to Emerson, "How plain that death is only the phenomenon of the individual or class. Nature does not recognize it, she finds her own again under new forms without loss. Yet death is beautiful when seen to be a law, and not an accident—It is as common as life. Men die in Tartary, in Ethiopia—in England—in Wisconsin. And after all what portion of this so serene and living nature can be said to be alive? Do this year's grasses and foliage outnumber all the past?

"Every blade in the field—every leaf in the forest—lays down its life in its season as beautifully as it was taken up. It is the pastime of a full quarter of the year. Dead trees—sere leaves—dried grass and herbs—are not these a good part of our life? And what is that pride of our autumnal scenery but the hectic flush—the sallow and cadaverous countenance of vegetation—its painted throes—with the November air for canvas—

"When we look over the fields are we not saddened because the particular flowers or grasses will wither—for the law of their death is the law of new life. Will not the land be in good heart *because* the crops die down from year to year? The herbage cheerfully consents to bloom, and wither, and give place to a new.

"So it is with the human plant. We are partial and selfish when we lament the death of the individual, unless our plaint be a paean to the departed soul, and a sigh as the wind sighs over the fields, which no shrub interprets into its private grief."

And under that same date—March 11, 1842—Thoreau cried out in his journal: "My life, my life! why will you linger? Are the years short and the months of no account? How often has long delay quenched my aspirations! Can God afford that I should forget him? . . . Why, God, did you include me in your great scheme? Will you not make me a partner at last?"

With John's death, Thoreau came to not only the fullest realization of the meaning of death, but also presently to acceptance of it—an experience which every young person must know at least once in his life, and one that comes usually with the death of someone dearly loved, as Thoreau loved his brother. The experience tempered him, but only confirmed him in his directions.

Meanwhile, the intellectuals were moving into Concord to add lustre to that village's fame. Bronson Alcott, with his wife, Abigail May, and their children, had come to live there in 1840. William Ellery Channing, nephew of Thoreau's professor of rhetoric, himself a poet, came with his bride, a sister of Margaret Fuller, to spend some time in the Emerson cottage in 1841. Since the cottage was on the grounds, it was inevitable that Thoreau should see something of him, though at this time Channing had come principally to see Emerson. It was only later that he became Thoreau's best friend, though in many ways Thoreau's opposite.

In September, 1841, Dr. Ezra Ripley died; he had been vaguely troubled by the Transcendental thinkers; he thought them "speculators" and not very firmly grounded. In the following July, Nathaniel Hawthorne and his wife, Sophia Peabody, came to live in the Old Manse. Emerson sent Thoreau to help put the garden in order. So the two men met, and, since both of them felt more kinship for the common man than the Transcendentalists, they became friends.

Hawthorne left in his notebook a description of Thoreau in 1842. He called him "a singular character; a young man with much of wild, original Nature still remaining in him; and so far as he is sophisticated, it is in a way and method of his own." He thought Thoreau ill-favored in looks—"long-nosed, queer-mouthed, and with uncouth and somewhat rustic manners. . . . But his ugliness is of an honest and agreeable fashion, and becomes him much better than beauty. . . . he has repudiated all regular means of getting a living, and seems inclined to lead a sort of Indian life. . . .

"He is a keen and delicate observer of Nature . . . a *genuine* observer, which I suspect is almost as rare a character as even an original poet. And Nature, in return for his love, seems to adopt him as her especial child; and shows him secrets which few others are allowed to witness. He is familiar with beast, fish, fowl and reptile, and has strange stories to tell of adventure and friendly passages with these lower brethren of mortality. Herb and flower, likewise, wherever they grow,

41

whether in garden or wildwood, are his familiar friends. He is on intimate terms with the clouds also, and can tell the portents of storms. He has a great regard for the memory of the Indian tribes, whose wild life would have suited him so well; and, strange to say, he seldom walks over a plowed field without picking up an arrowpoint, spearhead, or other relic of the red man. With all this he has more than a tincture of literature; a deep and true taste for poetry, especially for the elder poets; and he is a good writer. At least he has written a good article,—a rambling disquisition on Natural History, in the last *Dial,* which, he says, was chiefly made up from journals of his own observations. . . ."

Hawthorne's reference was to *The Natural History of Massachusetts,* which had just appeared in *The Dial,* in which in 1842 many of Thoreau's poems also appeared in print—*To the Maiden in the East, The Moon, The Summer Rain, To a Stray Fowl,* and others. As Hawthorne revealed, Thoreau was beginning now to draw upon his extensive journal for "pieces"—hardly essays—for the magazines which would publish them. There were not many such.

In mid-July of 1842 Thoreau took a long walk to Wachusett with Richard Fuller, Margaret Fuller's brother. This walk was later to become the subject of an article, and Thoreau kept an account of the journey. The two young men took their time, now and then resting on the rails of a fence, learning "that man's life is rounded with the same few facts, the same simple relations everywhere, and it is vain to travel to find it new." They stopped to bathe their feet in every brook, dawdled on every knoll, and spent their first night out at an inn four miles from the base of Wachusett.

Next morning before dawn, they began the climb of

Wachusett, following the Stillwater River to the mountain, gathering raspberries for breakfast. In this leisurely manner they reached the summit, which consisted "of a few acres, destitute of trees, covered with bare rocks, interspersed with blueberry bushes, raspberries, gooseberries, strawberries, moss, and a fine wiry grass. . . . This clear space, which is gently rounded, is bounded a few feet lower by a thick shrubbery of oaks, with maples, aspens, beeches, cherries, and occasionally a mountain-ash intermingled, among which we found the bright blue berries of the Solomon's seal, and the fruit of the pyrola."

They pitched their tent here, after which they had blueberries and milk for supper. "Before sunset, we rambled along the ridge to the north, while a hawk soared still above us. It was a place where gods might wander, so solemn and solitary, and removed from all contagion with the plain." By night, under the almost full moon, they strolled the summit and fed their spirits on the view. "There was, by chance, a fire blazing on Monadnock that night, which lighted up the whole western horizon, and, by making us aware of a community of mountains, made our position seem less solitary. . . . It was thrilling to hear the wind roar over the rocks . . . The night was, in its elements, simple even to majesty in that bleak place,— a bright moonlight and a piercing wind. It was at no time darker than twilight . . . and . . . there was the moon still above us, with Jupiter and Saturn on either hand, looking down on Wachusett, and it was a satisfaction to know that they were our fellow-travelers still, as high and out of our reach as our own destiny."

With moonset came the dawn. They were up before the sun, watching upon its rising, and taking in the splendid view. "We could see how ample and roomy is nature. . . . On every side, the eye ranged over successive circles of towns, rising one above another, like the terraces of a vineyard, till they were lost in the horizon. Wachusett is, in fact, the observatory of the State. There lay Massachusetts, spread out before us in its length and breadth, like a map. There was the level horizon, which told of the sea on the east and south, the well-known hills of New Hampshire on the north, and the misty summits of the Hoosac and Green Mountains, first made visible to us the evening before, blue and unsubstantial, like some bank of clouds which the morning wind would dissipate, on the northwest and west."

At noon they went back down the mountain, and, traveling with more dispatch, they reached Concord early the following morning. With scarcely any transition, Thoreau slipped back into his pattern—making pencils, continuing his sojourn at Emerson's, resuming his exploration of Concord town. From time to time he shared his company with Hawthorne and Emerson, as on the winter occasion when they went skating together and were later remembered by Rose Hawthorne Lathrop, Hawthorne's daughter, as a remarkable trio skating down the Concord River—Thoreau "an experienced skater—figuring dithyrambic dances and Bacchic leaps on the ice," Hawthorne "who, wrapped in his cloak, moved like a self-impelled Greek statue, stately and grave," and Emerson "too weary to hold himself erect, pitching headforemost, half lying on the air."

His journal grew in the sense that it was less derivative; he drew less upon other writers he read—save for the Hindus—and more upon himself, reflecting his attitudes. "I have been making pencils all day, and then at evening walked to see an old schoolmate who is going to help make the Welland Canal navigable for ships round

Niagara. He cannot see any such motives and modes of living as I; professes not to look beyond the securing of certain 'creature comforts.' And so we go silently different ways, with all serenity, I in the still moonlight through the village this fair evening to write these thoughts in my journal, and he, forsooth, to mature his schemes to ends as good, maybe, but different. So are we two made, while the same stars shine quietly over us. . . . So does the Welland Canal get built, and other conveniences, while I live. Well and good, I must confess. Fast sailing ships are hence not detained."

He linked his fate "in some sense" with the stars, "and if they are to persevere to a great end, shall I die who could conjecture it?" His association with the villagers opened to him many profound truths—"Man's moral nature is a riddle which only eternity can solve."—and, apart from expressing his dislikes and enthusiasms, he did not set himself in judgment upon his fellow citizens.

He had, too, already discerned an important fact about writing. "Those authors are successful who do not *write down* to others, but make their own taste and judgment their audience. By some strange infatuation we forget that we do not approve what yet we recommend to others. It is enough if I please myself with writing; I am then sure of an audience." And he had learned, too, that "Poetry cannot breathe in the scholar's atmosphere," and that "One does not soon learn the trade of life."

Despite the greater number of his contributions to *The Dial,* now that Emerson had assumed the editorship of that magazine, despite the security of his position, despite his freedom of movement, Thoreau was uncomfortable in his place in the Emerson household, and he evidently made Emerson, too, somewhat uncomfortable. Early in 1843 Hawthorne set down in his journal that

45

"Mr. Emerson seems to have suffered some inconvenience from his experience of Mr. Thoreau as an inmate. It may well be that such a sturdy, uncompromising person is fitter to meet occasionally in the open air than as a permanent guest at table and fireside." Thoreau, in short, was not a sycophant; he was not at Emerson's simply to agree with Emerson's propositions in an intellectual discussion; indeed, he was inclined rather to disagree. Emerson was frequently contradicted by Thoreau, and he found this somewhat wearing.

Well aware of Thoreau's desire to write and publish, Emerson enlisted his aid in the editing of *The Dial,* which he had taken over from Margaret Fuller early in 1842. The experience was salutary. With Emerson frequently away, Thoreau did more editing than he had contemplated—the entire April 1843 issue was edited by Thoreau, at about the same time—in February—that he wrote to Emerson that he was pondering "some other method of paying debts than by lectures and writing," and asking Emerson to look about in New York for something "of that 'other' sort" and "to remember it for me?"

Not long after, Emerson found some "other" occupation for Thoreau. It was as tutor to his brother William's son, Haven, on Staten Island. It was the kind of position which would put Thoreau next to the center of American publishing in New York. It would give him opportunity to meet editors and fellow writers other than those who belonged to the Concord group, though Thoreau had already met John O'Sullivan, one such editor—of *The Democratic Review*—at the Old Manse at Hawthorne's invitation earlier that year. Thoreau was promised board and room, as well as $100 a year—which was $100 more than he received at his present post.

On May 6, 1843, Thoreau left for Staten Island, by

boat. In a matter of days he was writing to "Dear Mother and Friends at Home," "I am seven and a half miles from New York, and, as it would take half a day at least, have not been there yet. I have already run over no small part of the island, to the highest hill, and some way along the shore. From the hill directly behind the house I can see New York, Brooklyn, Long Island, the Narrows, through which vessels bound to and from all parts of the world chiefly pass,—Sandy Hook and the Highlands of Neversink (part of the coast of New Jersey)—and, by going still farther up the hill, the Kill van Kull, and Newark Bay. From the pinnacle of one Madame Grimes' house the other night at sunset, I could see almost round the island. Far in the horizon there was a fleet of sloops bound up the Hudson, which seemed to be going over the edge of the earth, and in view of these trading ships, commerce seems quite imposing."

And he added, "But it is rather derogatory that your dwelling-place should be only a neighborhood to a great city,—to live on an inclined plane. I do not like their cities and forts, with their morning and evening guns, and sails flapping in one's eye. I want a whole continent to breathe in, and a good deal of solitude and silence, such as all Wall Street cannot buy,—nor Broadway with its wooden pavement. I must live along the beach, on the southern shore, which looks directly out to sea,—and see what that great parade of water means, that dashes and roars, and has not yet wet me, as long as I have lived. . . .

"I must not know anything about my condition and relations here till what is not permanent is worn off. I have not yet subsided. Give me time enough, and I may like it. . . . it will be long before I can make nature look as innocently grand and inspiring as in Concord."

47

Though he was by no means sure that Thoreau would ever find time enough to like any place but Concord, Emerson did everything he could to introduce Thoreau to the literary life of New York. On the day of his departure, he wrote a letter to the senior Henry James introducing Thoreau, and James immediately wrote to Thoreau at Staten Island inviting him to call at his convenience. After he had gone to New York—but not to see James—Thoreau wrote to Emerson, "You must not count much upon what I can do or learn in New York. I feel a good way off here . . . Everything there disappoints me but the crowd—rather I was disappointed with the rest before I came."

He was homesick for Concord and resumed the writing of poems, which he had abandoned for most of the time since John Thoreau's death. He did resolutely try, however, to meet people who might be of use to him. O'Sullivan, whom he had met at Hawthorne's Old Manse, bought *The Landlord* from him, and ordered a book review. He visited James early in June and liked him "very much. . . . I never was more kindly and faithfully catechised. It made me respect myself more to be thought worthy of such wise questions. He is a man, and takes his own way, or stands still in his own place." But on the whole, as he wrote to Emerson in the same letter in which he reported on James, "I always see those of whom I have heard well with a slight disappointment. They are so much better than the great herd, and yet the heavens are not shivered into diamonds over their heads." And, at the same time, he admitted, "I don't like the city better, the more I see it, but worse."

Of the people he thought genuine, and with whom he felt kinship—and there were not many in the setting where he found himself in 1843—there were two above all others—Henry James and Horace Greeley, who was to remain his friend for life, and who was to do all in his power to find an audience for him. Of the others, Thoreau thought but fleetingly. He tried every way he knew in which to increase his income—to make a living—even to selling subscriptions to *The Agriculturalist,* but he failed in all of them. As for his own writing, he wrote Emerson, "Literature comes to a poor market here, and even the little that I write is more than will sell."

He wrote many letters home—nostalgic letters. He wrote to his parents, to his sisters, to the Emersons, and their replies linked him to Concord. He came to Concord for Thanksgiving, returned briefly to Staten Island, and then finally, Concord being more vital to him than any other place, he returned to his home place early in December. There he meant to stay.

CHAPTER 4

A Place of His Own

> *I went to the woods because I wished to live de-*
> *liberately, to front only the essential facts of life,*
> *and see if I could not learn what it had to teach,*
> *and not, when I came to die, discover that I had*
> *not lived. I did not wish to live what was not life,*
> *living is so dear; nor did I wish to practise resigna-*
> *tion, unless it was quite necessary. I wanted to live*
> *deep and suck out all the marrow of life, to live so*
> *sturdily and Spartan-like as to put to rout all that*
> *was not life, to cut a broad swath and shave close,*
> *to drive life into a corner, and reduce it to its lowest*
> *terms, and, if it proved to be mean, why then to get*
> *the whole and genuine meanness of it, and publish*
> *its meanness to the world; or if it were sublime, to*
> *know it by experience, and be able to give a true*
> *account of it in my next excursion.* —WALDEN

HE settled back into life in Concord as easily as if he had never left it, as if he had
gone to Staten Island with no intention of remaining away
from the place he liked best of all those he had known, and
wished to know no other. He had told George Ward in
New York that, having studied books, he now meant to
study nature and his fellowmen, and he set about it. He
was back at making pencils once more, and he was occupied in helping his father to build a house across the new
railroad tracks which had been put in from Boston through
to Fitchburg. This house was called the "Texas house,"

50

either because it was so far from the Mill Dam or because of the current agitation of the Texas question. The Thoreaus had been building it, off and on, for three years.

He resumed his exploratory acquaintance with the woods, the rivers, the fields and ponds, very often alone, but sometimes with William Ellery Channing, who had come to live in Concord, or with Emerson, and perhaps on occasion with his idealistic friend, Isaac Hecker, who was studying Latin and Greek under the schoolmaster, George Bradford, in Concord, and rooming at the Thoreau house. Channing was a lively companion, in many ways the opposite of Thoreau. He was gay, witty, much given to flowery speech and not above telling a risque story once in a while, perhaps as much to annoy Thoreau as to entertain himself, for Thoreau frowned on levity in dealing with matters of sex.

On Town Meeting day that April of 1844, Edward Hoar, home from studying at Harvard, went along with Thoreau on a trip up the Sudbury River, and, having caught some fish, the two stopped along shore to fry them. They took the usual precautions, but the day was a windy one, and the grass along the edge of the woods caught fire. They had intended to camp out, but the fire drove all else from their minds. They tried to stamp it out, then got a board from the boat and tried to beat out the flames, to no avail. The wind spread the flames along the hillside away from Fair Haven Pond.

While the flames would be halted on one side by the Well Meadow Brook, there was a distinct possibility that they might get to Concord on the other. Edward Hoar took the boat down river, and Thoreau ran through the woods to arouse the town. On the way, he met the owner of the woods, and told him what had happened; the two ran all the way back to the scene, meeting a carpenter who had been driven from the woods by the approaching flames. He went on to give the alarm, together with the owner; Thoreau, tired from running, stayed behind. "What could I do alone against a front of flame half a mile wide?" he asked when at last he recorded the incident in his journal six years later.

He climbed to the highest rock on Fair Haven Cliff and sat down to watch the flames move toward him. They had by this time traveled a mile. The alarm bell rang, and Thoreau knew that help was on the way. "Hitherto I had felt like a guilty person," he wrote in his journal, "—nothing but shame and regret. But now I settled the matter with myself shortly. I said to myself: 'Who are these men who are said to be the owners of these woods, and how am I related to them? I have set fire to the forest, but I have done no wrong therein, and now it is as if the lightning had done it. These flames are but consuming their natural food.' (It has never troubled me from that day to this more than if the lightning had done it. The trivial fishing was all that disturbed me and disturbs me still.)"

Pressed by the approach of the fire at last, Thoreau went down to join the fire-fighters reaching the scene from Concord. For several hours they fought the flames with hoes, shovels, and back fires. Before they had contained it, the fire had burned over a hundred acres of woodland.

The experience was instructive for Thoreau. "When I returned home late in the day, with others of my townsmen, I could not help noticing that the crowd who were so ready to condemn the individual who had kindled the fire did not sympathize with the owners of the wood, but were in fact highly elate and as it were thankful for the opportunity which had afforded them so much sport; and it was only half a dozen owners, so called, though not all of them, who looked sour or grieved, and I felt that I had a deeper interest in the woods, knew them better and should feel their loss more, than any or all of them." At least one of his townsmen called Thoreau a "damned rascal."

That night Thoreau returned to the woods to wander through them, among the burning stumps, and "far in the night I threaded my way to the spot where the fire had taken, and discovered the now broiled fish . . . scattered over the burnt grass." What his inmost thoughts were as he walked through the blackened waste is not recorded. One can imagine them. He who had loved the woods had, even if by accident, destroyed them.

More important, the incident showed him the Thoreau his townsmen saw. He regarded himself as an individual, a nonconformist in thought. At this point he must have learned that his fellow townsmen looked upon him as an eccentric, more or less a loafer, and, to cap this low opinion, as an irresponsible rascal. This is the kind of discovery almost every creative solitary sooner or later makes when some such incident brings him face to face with what has been smoldering in the thoughts of his fellowmen for a long time.

In subsequent days, as he walked the familiar Concord streets and lanes, he learned to grow accustomed to anonymous jeers and shouts sent toward his retreating back. "Burnt woods!" some of his fellow townsmen called after him. It must have hardened a resolve which had long been growing in him—to put a little distance between his townsmen and himself. This had been a goal ever since he had failed to acquire the Hollowell Farm, and as the year wore on, he came closer and closer to it.

Isaac Hecker left Concord and made his way into the Catholic religion, asking Thoreau to go on a hiking tour of the Continent with him. Thoreau declined. But that summer he went on a walking tour of the Berkshires and the Catskills with Channing. When his friend Emerson announced an address—*On the Anniversary of the Emancipation of the Negroes in the British West Indies*—and the Concord churches, with that timidity which always afflicts settled social units at any criticism of the status quo, refused the use of their buildings for this purpose, Thoreau managed to persuade the authorities to permit Emerson use of the Concord courthouse. Thoreau himself rang the bell to announce to Concord the hour of the address, delivered on August 1, 1844.

Thoreau's disaffection with his fellow townsmen—or, more importantly, their attitude toward him—was aggravated by the end of *The Dial* and the consequent closing of an outlet for Thoreau's writing. The last volume had contained his essay, *A Winter Walk*. There was no other magazine of the day which was inclined to look favorably upon Thoreau's work. It was time for Thoreau to take stock of himself, to find opportunity to prepare a book which had been in his thoughts ever since his brother's death.

The opportunity lay before him. In October of that year Emerson bought eleven acres of land along the shores of Walden Pond. He wrote his brother William that "As . . . for years I had a sort of daily occupancy in it, I bid on it and bought it, eleven acres, for $8.10 per acre." Shortly after, he bought a few more acres of adjoining woodland from Heartwell Bigelow—a woodlot of scrub pine, white pines, briars, blackberries. Channing had once called the place "Briars" and Emerson also referred to its thorny nature. But Channing thought it might be ideal for Thoreau to occupy. "I see nothing for you in this earth but that field which I once christened 'Briars'; go out upon that, build yourself a hut, and there begin the grand process of devouring yourself alive," he wrote to Thoreau early in March, 1845. A little farther along in this letter he refers satirically to Thoreau in the third person as "too dry, too confused, too chalky, too concrete."

The idea of a retreat at Walden Pond fitted in with Thoreau's scheme of things. This was only another version of the "garret" he constantly sought; it was, in effect, an attic room in an ideal setting. Emerson was delighted with the idea of having Thoreau once more as a tenant, albeit two miles off where his social truculence would hardly be apparent to the talkers who gathered at Emerson's Concord house. Before the end of that month, Thoreau began to clear the briars from the field above Walden. In his own way, he was already paying rent on the land he hoped to occupy.

"It was a pleasant hillside where I worked, covered with pine woods, through which I looked out on the pond, and a small open field in the woods where pines and hickories were springing up. The ice in the pond was not yet dissolved, though there were some open spaces, and it was all dark-colored and saturated with water." He walked to and from Concord on the Fitchburg railroad, which ran along the west end of the pond, though his site was closer to the road that ran along the east end toward Cambridge.

"So I went on for some days cutting and hewing timber, and also studs and rafters, all with my narrow axe, not having many communicable or scholar-like thoughts, singing to myself,—

Men say they know many things;
But lo! they have taken wings,—
The arts and sciences,
And a thousand appliances:
The wind that blows
Is all that anybody knows.

I hewed the main timbers six inches square, most of the studs on two sides only, and the rafters and floor timbers on one side, leaving the rest of the bark on, so that they were just as straight and much stronger than sawed ones. Each stick was carefully mortised or tenoned by its stump, for I had borrowed other tools by this time. My days in the woods were not very long ones; yet I usually carried my dinner of bread and butter, and read the newspaper in which it was wrapped, at noon, sitting amid the green pine boughs which I had cut off, and to my bread was imparted some of their fragrance, for my hands were covered with a thick coat of pitch. . . . Sometimes a rambler in the wood was attracted by the sound of my axe, and we chatted pleasantly over the chips which I had made.

"By the middle of April, for I made no haste in my work, but rather made the most of it, my house was framed and ready for the raising. I had already bought the shanty of James Collins, an Irishman who worked on the Fitchburg Railroad, for boards. James Collins' shanty was considered an uncommonly fine one. . . . I took down this dwelling . . . drawing the nails, and removed it to the pond-side by small cartloads, spreading the boards on the grass there to bleach and warp back again in the sun. . . .

"I dug my cellar in the side of a hill sloping to the south, where a woodchuck had formerly dug his burrow, down through sumach and blackberry roots, and the lowest stain of vegetation, six feet square by seven deep, to a fine sand where potatoes would not freeze in any winter. The sides were left shelving, and not stoned; but the sun having never shone on them, the sand still keeps its place. It was but two hours' work. I took particular pleasure in this breaking of ground, for in almost all latitudes men dig into the earth for an equable temperature. . . .

"At length, in the beginning of May, with the help of some of my acquaintances . . . I set up the frame of my house. No man was ever more honored in the character of his raisers than I." The men who helped him in this were his friend Channing, George William Curtis, who was then living with Edmund Hosmer, Bronson Alcott, and Hosmer himself. The cabin cost Thoreau $28.12½, by his own careful reckoning.

Channing wrote of it, "As for its being in the ordinary meaning a house, it was so superior to the common domestic contrivances that I do not associate it with them. By standing on a chair you could reach into the garret, and a corn broom fathomed the depth of the cellar. It had no lock to the door, no curtain to the window, and belonged to nature nearly as much as to man. . . . It was just large enough for one, like the plate of boiled apple pudding he used to order of the restauranteur. . . . It was . . . a sentry-box in the shore, in the wood of Walden, ready to walk into in rain or snow or cold. . . ."

Into this cabin Thoreau moved a bed, a desk, a table, a few utensils, three chairs, and a tiny looking-glass but three inches in diameter. One of the chairs Thoreau used for the purpose of announcing that he was open to visitors by dint of setting the chair outside his door. On the fourth of July, 1845, Thoreau moved into the cabin on the shore of the cove on the north side of Walden Pond. Two days later he wrote in his journal:

"I wish to meet the facts of life—the vital facts, which are the phenomena of actuality the gods meant to show us—face to face, and so I came down here. Life! who knows what it is, what it does? If I am not quite right here, I am less wrong than before; and now let us see what they will have."

He set about his business at Walden Pond without delay. He had his previous journals with him—and the material he wished to draw upon to write *A Week on the Concord and Merrimack Rivers*—the two weeks he had spent on this excursion with his brother he saw best as a week for the purposes of his account, which was to be much more than a simple record of the journey. At the same time he was putting down his notes for *Walden,* however unconsciously.

He reveled in his freedom, in his solitude—which was not quite the solitude of a recluse, for the retreat at Walden Pond was not a hermitage. He was visited by Hosmer, Alex Therien, a garrulous wood-chopper, Channing, members of his family, and others; he walked into Concord whenever the mood was upon him—for conversation, or to find some food not of his own baking—for he baked bread for himself at his own hearth—or to see people or to attend a lecture at the Lyceum. He did not pretend to be a hermit. He had but established a listening post in a familiar wilderness with one foot, as it were, on the threshold of the village, so that he could withdraw in either direction, as his inclination dictated.

He accepted his animal neighbors and they accepted him. A mouse nested under his house "and came when I took my luncheon to pick the crumbs at my feet. It had never seen the race of man before, and so the sooner became familiar. It ran over my shoes and up my pantaloons inside, clinging to my flesh with its sharp claws. It would run up the side of the room by short impulses like a squirrel. . . . At length, as I leaned my elbow on the bench, it ran over my arm and round the paper which contained my dinner. And when I held it a piece of cheese, it came and nibbled between my fingers, and then cleaned its face and paws like a fly."

He sat outside of evenings and played his flute and heard the echo from a nearby wood—"a stolen pleasure, occasionally not rightfully heard, much more for other ears than ours," and pondered his position: "A man must find his own occasion in himself. The natural day is very calm, and will hardly reprove our indolence. If there is no elevation in our spirits, the pond will not seem elevated like a mountain tarn, but a low pool, a silent muddy water, a place for fishermen.

"I sit here at my window like a priest of Isis, and observe the phenomena of three thousand years ago, yet unimpaired. The tantivy of wild pigeons, an ancient race of birds, gives a voice to the air, flying by twos and threes athwart my view or perching restless on the white pine boughs occasionally; a fish hawk dimples the glassy surface of the pond and brings up a fish; and for the last half-hour I have heard the rattle of railroad cars conveying travellers from Boston to the country."

He spent a little while from time to time tending his "garden." Even before he had finished his house, "wishing to earn ten or twelve dollars by some honest and agreeable method, in order to meet my unusual expenses," he had planted over two acres in beans, with a small part reserved for potatoes, corn, peas, and turnips. He did not "quite hoe it all once. I got out several cords of stumps in plowing, which supplied me with

59

fuel for a long time, and left small circles of virgin mold, easily distinguishable through the summer by the greater luxuriance of the beans there. . . . I was obliged to hire a team and a man for the plowing, though I held the plow myself. My farm outgoes for the first season were, for implements, seed, work, etc., $14.72½. The seed corn was given me. This never costs anything to speak of, unless you plant more than enough. I got twelve bushels of beans, and eighteen bushels of potatoes, beside some peas and sweet corn. The yellow corn and turnips were too late to come to anything."

His net income from the venture at farming was $8.71½ "beside produce consumed and on hand at the time this estimate was made of the value of $4.50,—the amount on hand more than balancing a little grass which I did not raise. All things considered, that is, considering the importance of a man's soul and of to-day, notwithstanding the short time occupied by my experiment, nay, partly even because of its transient character, I believe that that was doing better than any farmer in Concord did that year."

Whatever his townsmen thought of his venture—and among them, Channing had spent some months in a hut on the Illinois prairies—he himself did not think that he had gone into any wilderness to live in isolation. "It is in vain to dream of a wildness distant from ourselves. . . . I shall never find in the wilds of Labrador any greater wildness than in some recess in Concord, i.e., than I import into it." The townsmen—save for Alcott, Emerson and Channing—saw no evidence that Thoreau at Walden Pond was other than a farmer, in a small way; the creative life seldom leaves evidence of work immediately apparent, as, for instance, the mound of earth left by a ditch-digger.

His chief concern at Walden was not, after all, raising beans. It was in a sense an attempt to justify his way of life—the rightness of doing what he wanted. In the course of it he intensified his study of nature and of man—just as he had said he would do—not so much the men of Concord village, whom he had known before, as the men who were his fellows in the wilder areas of the town—Alex Therien ("a Canadian now, a woodchopper, a post-maker . . . and who made his last supper on a woodchuck which his dog caught")—to whom Thoreau occasionally read—the Irish laborers settled in the vicinity after building the railroad, among them John Field, and Hugh Quoil ("He was a man of manners and gentlemanlike, as one who had seen the world, and was capable of more civil speech than you could well attend to.").

In the course of his enquiry he also worked on his first book.

He had begun the writing of *A Week on the Concord and Merrimack Rivers* even before moving to Walden. As early as March, 1845, he had delivered before the Concord Lyceum as a lecture the opening chapter of that book, *Concord River,* and he now set himself to raiding his earlier journal for the material to round out the book so begun. He intended it to be a compendium of verse, quotations, essays all hung loosely within the frame of a seven-day excursion on the Musketaquid or Grassgrown River now called the Concord.

Since the early journal was filled with quotations, there was no dearth of them. He began by quoting Ovid and ended with Virgil; between them he used Donne, Pindar, Spenser, Emerson, Chaucer, Channing, Quarles, Bishop Percy, Anacreon, Tennyson, George Herbert, and others. Within the frame of the excursion he had taken with his brother, he set down whatever seized his fancy,

61

taking off from paragraphs in the early journals. He included no less than half a hundred of his own poems or fragments of poems. He put in essays on prose, on Christianity, friendship, history, satire. Yet, while the title he chose for his book invited prospective readers to join him and his brother on a leisurely trip on the rivers, it was his primary purpose to offer his essays in some acceptable frame. These little essays, so carefully wrought, were for Thoreau the heart and substance of this first book he put together.

The book occupied him, but not exclusively. He found time to tend his beans—but less in the spring of 1846, when the book was nearing completion, and when he recorded that he planted fewer beans and more "sincerity, truth, simplicity, faith, innocence," which may have been a reference to the work in progress. He found time to prepare material for his most unified and best work, yet to come, and to write *Thomas Carlyle and His Works* ("It is not in man to determine what his style shall be. He might as well determine what his thoughts shall be. . . . No, his thoughts were ever irregular and impetuous. . . . Who cares what a man's style is, so it is intelligible,—as intelligible as his thought. Literally and really, the style is no more than the *stylus*, the pen he writes with; and it is not worth scraping and polishing, and gilding, unless it will write his thoughts the better for it. It is something for use, and not to look at. . . . Translate a book a dozen times from one language to another, and what becomes of its style? . . . We believe that Carlyle has, after all, more readers, and is better known to-day for this very originality of style, and that posterity will have reason to thank him for emancipating the language, in some measure, from the fetters which a merely conservative, aimless, and pedantic literary class had imposed upon it, and setting an example of greater freedom and naturalness.")

Like most authors, he tried out selected portions of his book on his visitors. Bronson Alcott was especially impressed by what he heard in the course of his various visits to the cabin at Walden. In his own journal, Alcott wrote, "The book is purely American, fragrant with the lives of New England woods and streams, and could have been written nowhere else. . . . There is a toughness too, and a sinewy vigor, as of roots and the strength that comes of feeding on wild meats, and the moist lustres of the fishes in the bed below. It has the merit, moreover, that somehow, despite all presumptions to the contrary, the sod and sap and fibre and flavor of New England have found at last a clear relation to the literature of other and classic lands."

He read part of the book to Emerson, "under an oak on the river bank the other afternoon," as Emerson wrote. "In a short time, if Wiley and Putnam smile, you shall have Henry Thoreau's *Excursion on the Concord and Merrimack Rivers,* a seven days' voyage in as many chapters, pastoral as Isaak Walton, spicy as flagroot, broad and deep as Menu. He read me some of it . . . and invigorated me." Emerson's reference was to a firm of New York publishers with which he was acquainted. At the time of this letter—July, 1846—the book was ready for publication, though it was yet to undergo further revision.

Thoreau had high hopes for it. What budding author does not have such hopes for his first book?—unaware of the often painful realities of publishing, which are so different from what the author conceives them to be. Very probably Emerson himself sent it off to Wiley and Putnam. Thoreau had some reason to be hopeful, for, through the good offices of Horace Greeley, he soon learned that he had been accepted elsewhere.

Greeley, impressed by his essay on Carlyle, had undertaken to send it around, and presently wrote to say that Rufus Griswold, editor of *Graham's Magazine,* had accepted it for his magazine "to be paid for at the usual rate." Thoreau began to feel that a way to maintain himself in his modest way was being opened for him by his pen, and he entertained visions of a large edition of his first book at a popular price, so that it might have a wide circulation. He waited for Wiley and Putnam to smile upon his fledgeling.

He waited in vain.

CHAPTER 5

Journey to Maine

The authority of government, even such as I am willing to submit to—for I will cheerfully obey those who know and can do better than I, and in many things even those who neither know nor can do so well—is still an impure one: to be strictly just, it must have the sanction and consent of the governed. It can have no pure right over my person and property but what I concede to it. The progress from an absolute to a limited monarchy, from a limited monarchy to a democracy, is a progress toward a true respect for the individual. Even the Chinese philosopher was wise enough to regard the individual as the basis of the empire. Is a democracy, such as we know it, the last improvement possible in government? Is it not possible to take a step further towards recognizing and organizing the rights of man? There will never be a really free and enlightened State until the State comes to recognize the individual as a higher and independent power, from which all its own power and authority are derived, and treats him accordingly. I please myself with imagining a State at least which can afford to be just to all men, and to treat the individual with respect as a neighbor; which even would not think it inconsistent with its own repose if a few were to live aloof from it, not meddling with it, nor embraced by it, who fulfilled all the duties of neighbors and fellow-men. A State which bore this kind of fruit, and suffered it to drop off as fast as it ripened, would prepare the way for a still more perfect and glorious State, which also I have imagined, but not yet anywhere seen. —CIVIL DISOBEDIENCE

ONE July evening in 1846, planning to go berrying next day, Thoreau walked into Concord from Walden to get a shoe he had left at the cobbler's for mending. He was accosted by Sam Staples, the Concord jailer, and charged with not having paid his poll tax. Thoreau had not paid poll tax since 1843— when Bronson Alcott had spent a night in jail for refusing to pay his. Why should he? He had never voted, and such a purely political tax as a poll tax was allied to such political acts as the Mexican War, which had begun that May, and the maintenance of slavery.

Without more ado, Thoreau was clapped into jail, "mad as the devil," as Staples recalled it later. His anger cooled. He heard Staples lock up, take off his boots, and close the jail for the night. Here Thoreau was, and here he had to stay. He grew philosophical.

"As I stood considering the walls of solid stone, two or three feet thick, the door of wood and iron, a foot thick, and the iron grating which strained the light, I could not help being struck with the foolishness of that institution which treated me as if I were mere flesh and blood and bones, to be locked up. I wondered that it should have concluded at length that this was the best use it could put me to, and had never thought to avail itself of my services in some way. I saw that, if there was a wall of stone between me and my townsmen, there was a still more difficult one to climb or break through before they could get to be as free as I was. I did not for a moment feel confined, and the walls seemed a great waste of stone and mortar. I felt as if I alone of all my towns-

66

men had paid my tax. . . . I could not but smile to see how industriously they locked the door on my meditations, which followed them out again without let or hindrance, and *they* were really all that was dangerous. . . .

"It was like travelling into a far country, such as I had never expected to behold, to lie there for one night. It seemed to me that I never had heard the town clock strike before, nor the evening sounds of the village; for we slept with the windows open, which were inside the grating. It was to see my native village in the light of the Middle Ages, and our Concord was turned into a Rhine stream, and visions of knights and castles passed before me. They were the voices of old burghers that I heard in the streets. I was an involuntary spectator and auditor of whatever was done and said in the kitchen of the adjacent village inn—a wholly new and rare experience to me. It was a closer view of my native town. I was fairly inside of it. I never had seen its institutions before. This is one of its peculiar institutions; for it is a shire town. I began to comprehend what its inhabitants were about.

"In the morning, our breakfasts were put through the hole in the door, in small oblong-square tin pans, made to fit, and holding a pint of chocolate, with brown bread, and an iron spoon. When they called for the vessels again, I was green enough to return what bread I had left; but my comrade seized it, and said that I should lay that up for lunch or dinner. . . .

"I saw yet more distinctly the State in which I lived. I saw to what extent the people among whom I lived could be trusted as good neighbors and friends; that their friendship was for summer weather only . . ."

Some years previous to Thoreau's imprisonment, he had "signed off" from his church affiliation. "The State met me in behalf of the Church, and commanded me to pay a certain sum toward the support of a clergyman whose preaching my father attended, but never I myself. . . . I declined to pay. . . . However, at the request of the selectmen, I condescended to make some such statement as this in writing:—'Know all men by these presents, that I, Henry Thoreau, do not wish to be regarded as a member of any incorporated society which I have not joined.' This I gave to the town clerk; and he has it. The State, having thus learned that I did not wish to be regarded as a member of that church, has never made a like demand on me since. . . ."

In prison, Thoreau made friends with his cell-mate; Staples told Thoreau that he was "a first-rate fellow and a clever man." He had been put into prison accused of arson, but Thoreau was of the opinion that "he had probably gone to bed in a barn when drunk, and smoked his pipe there; and so a barn was burnt." He pumped his fellow-prisoner "as dry as I could," but eventually they turned in.

In the morning Thoreau was released because some-one—probably his Aunt Maria Thoreau—had paid his tax. He was even angrier at this. His fellow townsmen "first looked at me, and then at one another, as if I had returned from a long journey." Undoubtedly they were not as surprised as Thoreau thought they might be, for patently a fellow who did nothing much but walk around and make notes in his journal, with enough time to set the woods on fire, instead of being engaged in some socially approved venture which would make him money, could be expected to land in jail sooner or later.

Once released, Thoreau went on about his business. He had been on his way for a mended shoe; so he got it. He had intended to lead a berrying party into the hills and in half an hour he was "on one of our highest hills, two miles off, and then the State was nowhere to be seen."

Out of this experience grew his first statement of his individual philosophy, originally titled *Resistance to Civil Government,* and written two years after, at almost the same time that Karl Marx was setting down *The Communist Manifesto.* But Thoreau's concern was with principles, not the reform of society, and he celebrated the individuality of man and the problems which do not yield to solution by any political structure or philosophy.

The imprisonment left an indelible impression on Thoreau. He could be amused by it later, but he thought about the principles involved a long time, for it was almost two years before he wrote about it in the essay which was eventually to be titled *Civil Disobedience.* It was not such a paper as would inflame to mass rebellion, but only an account of the individual of integrity, who has no recourse but to oppose the oppression of the State by means of passive resistance.

"Action from principle . . . changes things and relations; it is essentially revolutionary," he wrote when in retrospect he considered his arrest and the reasons for it. "If the injustice is part of the necessary friction of the machine of government, let it go, let it go: perchance it will wear smooth. . . . But if it is of such a nature that it requires you to be the agent of injustice to another, then, I say, break the law. . . . I was not born to be forced. I will breathe after my own fashion. . . . If a plant cannot live according to its nature, it dies; and so a man. . . . I am as desirous of being a good neighbor as I am of being a bad subject."

For the nonce, however, he was berry-picking, heading a party in the hills, and presently, finishing with this, he walked back to Walden and resumed where he had left off—the affairs which had brought him to this place, which now included the beginnings of his second book, *Walden*. This did not occupy him so exclusively that he found it impossible to leave the area; on the last day of August, 1846, he set out for a trip through Maine.

"I left Concord . . . for Bangor and the backwoods of Maine, by way of the railroad and steamboat, intending to accompany a relative of mine . . . as far as a dam on the west branch of the Penobscot. . . . From this place, which is about one hundred miles by the river above Bangor, I proposed to make excursions to Mount Ktaadn, the second highest mountain in New England, . . . and to some of the lakes of the Penobscot, either alone or with such company as I might pick up there."

In Maine, as was the case wherever he went, Thoreau set down voluminous notes. Everything was grist for him. He went, as always, in wonder, clear-eyed, anxious to miss no detail which might enlarge his horizons or add to his knowledge of nature and his fellowmen, and enable him to draw sound conclusions about man and his place in the universe. Whatever he saw might be turned into lectures, articles for the magazines, or perhaps even a book.

He was prepared to learn more about the Indians and how they lived, for the Penobscots roamed the Maine wilderness. He hoped to study them at first hand, but the Indian guides who had been arranged for, did not show up, and George McCauslin was persuaded to take the party instead. "McCauslin was a Kennebec man, of Scotch descent, who had been a waterman twenty-two years, and had driven on the lakes and headwaters of the Penobscot five or six springs in succession, but was now settled here to raise supplies for the lumberers and for himself. . . . A man of dry wit and shrewdness, and

70

a general intelligence which I had not looked for in the backwoods. In fact, the deeper you penetrate into the woods, the more intelligent, and, in one sense, less countrified do you find the inhabitants; for always the pioneer has been a traveler, and, to some extent, a man of the world; and, as the distances with which he is familiar are greater, so is his information more general and far reaching than the villagers'. If I were to look for a narrow, uninformed, and countrified mind, as opposed to the intelligence and refinement which are thought to emanate from cities, it would be among the rusty inhabitants of an old-settled country, on farms all run out and gone to seed with life-everlasting, in the towns about Boston, even on the high-road in Concord, and not in the backwoods of Maine."

They went into country of bear and moose and added to their supplies by fishing. "Seizing the birch poles which some party of Indians, or white hunters, had left on the shore, and baiting our hooks with pork, and with trout, as soon as they were caught, we cast our lines into the mouth of the Aboljacknagesic, a clear, swift, shallow stream, which came in from Ktaadn. Instantly a shoal of white chivlin (*Leucisci pulchelli*), silvery roaches, cousin-trout, or what not, large and small, prowling thereabouts, fell upon our bait, and one after another were landed amidst the bushes. Anon their cousins, the true trout, took their turn, and alternately the speckled trout, and the silvery roaches, swallowed the bait as fast as we could throw in; and the finest specimens of both that I have ever seen, the largest one weighing three pounds, were heaved upon the shore . . . While yet alive, before their tints had faded, they glistened like the fairest flowers, the product of primitive rivers; and (the angler) could hardly trust his senses, as he stood

71

over them, that these jewels should have swam away in that Aboljacknagesic water for so long, so many dark ages;—these bright fluviatile flowers, seen of Indians only, made beautiful, the Lord only knows why, to swim there! I could understand better for this, the truth of mythology, the fables of Proteus, and all those beautiful sea-monsters,—how all history, indeed, put to a terrestrial use, is mere history; but put to a celestial, is mythology always."

The party traveled until they broke a pike-pole and ran short of provisions, then turned back. Thoreau was so favorably impressed with the Maine woods that he resolved to return, if opportunity came. "What is most striking in the Maine wilderness is the continuousness of the forest, with fewer open intervals or glades than you had imagined. Except the few burnt lands, the narrow intervals on the rivers, the bare tops of the high mountains, and the lakes and streams, the forest is uninterrupted. It is even more grim and wild than you had anticipated, a damp and intricate wilderness, in the spring everywhere wet and miry. The aspect of the country, indeed, is universally stern and savage, excepting the distant views of the forest from hills, and the lake prospects, which are mild and civilizing in a degree. . . . The aborigines have never been dispossessed, nor nature disforested. . . .

"What a place to live, what a place to die and be buried in! There certainly men would live forever, and laugh at death and the grave. . . .

"I am reminded by my journey how exceedingly new this country still is. You have only to travel for a few days into the interior and back parts even of many of the old States, to come to that very America which the Northmen, and Cabot, and Gosnold, and Smith, and Raleigh visited. If Columbus was the first to discover the islands,

72

Americus Vespucius and Cabot, and the Puritans, and we their descendants, have discovered only the shores of America."

Back in Concord, he took up where he had left off—at Walden. No matter how much he might move out from the cabin along the shore of the pond, this was his retreat where he might come face to face with himself. He continued to write, perhaps with a certain desperation. He was now in his thirtieth year, he had yet to have a book published, and his magazine appearances, apart from *The Dial,* were few and far between. He worked at *Walden,* and from his journal drew material for lectures to be given at the Concord Lyceum, and, hopefully, elsewhere at a fee.

In February, 1847, he lectured twice at the Lyceum—once *The History of Myself,* the second time on *Walden,* and his life there; these were the first public revelation of any part of that second book. But his primary concern was still publication, and he must have been understandably nettled at the lack of it—his first book had yet to find a publisher, and *Graham's Magazine* had not yet printed his *Thomas Carlyle and His Works.*

He wrote to Wiley & Putnam asking that his book manuscript be sent back so that he could revise it yet again, and he wrote to Horace Greeley to suggest withdrawal of his article from *Graham's.* Greeley replied in haste to say that the article was in type and destined for the leading place in the March issue of the magazine, and to beg Thoreau not to be "unreasonably sensitive at the delay." He was somewhat troubled by Thoreau's suggestion that the article be withdrawn and pointed out to him the advantages of appearing in a magazine with so much prestige as *Graham's.* At the same time, he suggested to Thoreau that he might soon have material enough for a volume worth publishing, and promised to "see what can be done" about publishing it. He also offered to publish any article Thoreau might care to write about Emerson or Hawthorne, and pay him well for it; but Thoreau was deaf to this offer because he would not take advantage of friendship for money.

He had, this year, at least one different commission. When Horatio B. Storer, a young naturalist studying at Harvard, asked him whether he collected specimens of birds' eggs, Thoreau confessed "to a little squeamishness on the score of robbing their nests, though I could easily go to the length of abstracting an egg or two gently, now and then, and if the advancement of science obviously demanded it might be carried even to the extreme of deliberate murder." But he was less loath to collect live specimens for Louis Agassiz, who had come to Harvard from Switzerland to lecture, beginning in October, 1846. By way of his friend, James Cabot, Thoreau sent to Agassiz a collection of fish, turtles, a black snake, and a mouse he had put together at Walden.

Cabot reported that Agassiz was delighted with the specimens and would like to see more. Some money was paid to Thoreau for them, but it was very probably paid to cover expenses incurred in obtaining them. That spring of 1847 Thoreau gathered many fish and reptiles and sent them to Agassiz through Cabot. He suggested that Agassiz himself might like to come to Walden for "a spearing excursion," but his lectures so occupied Agassiz that he could not accept Thoreau's invitation to join him.

In May Thoreau sent Cabot a long letter listing the fish commonly found in the Concord waters—pickerel ("Those caught in Walden, hard by my house, are easily distinguished from those caught in the river, being much heavier in proportion to their size, stouter, firmer fleshed, and lighter colored. The little pickerel which I sent last, jumped into the boat in its fright."), pouts, breams ("Some more green, others more brown."), suckers, perch ("I have counted ten transverse bands on some of the smaller."), lampreys ("Very scarce since the dams at Lowell and Billerica were built."), shiners, roach or chiverin, trout, eels, and red-finned minnows ("I have never recognized them in any books. Have they any scientific name?"), and asked, "What of the above does M. Agassiz particularly wish to see?" Agassiz particularly wished to see "the pickerel with the long snout, which he suspects may be the *Esox estor,* or Maskalongé."

On June 1, Thoreau sent in "15 pouts, 17 perch, 13 shiners, 1 larger land tortoise, and 5 muddy tortoises . . . 7 perch, 5 shiners, 8 breams, 4 dace? 2 muddy tortoises, 5 painted do., and 3 land do." variously from Walden Pond and the river. He sent also "one black snake, alive, and one dormouse? caught last night in my cellar," and promised to send "the pickerel with the longer snout" when he met with it. He was anxious to have for himself any scientific information about the specimens which he himself did not yet have, and was as delighted as Agassiz to learn that he had probably turned up one or two new species.

Meanwhile, Thoreau's first book was going the rounds of the publishers in vain. By late August Thoreau was inquiring of James Munroe & Company how much it would cost to publish the book at his own expense. And on September 6 of that year he left the Walden cabin as abruptly as he had come to it. "There was a little stagnation, it may be. About 2 o'clock in the afternoon the world's axle creaked as if it needed greasing. . . . I left the woods for as good a reason as I went there. Perhaps it seemed to me that I had several more lives to live, and could not spare any more time for that one. It is remarkable how easily and insensibly we fall into a particular route, and make a beaten track for ourselves. I had not lived there a week before my feet wore a path from my door to the pond-side . . . I did not wish to take a cabin passage, but rather to go before the mast and on the deck of the world, for there I could best see the moonlight amid the mountains. I do not wish to go below now."

Within a month, Thoreau was once more at the room at the head of the stairs in Emerson's house—invited to stay there by Lidian Emerson with Emerson's approval while Emerson himself went on a lecture tour of England. And that autumn, too, he cut the tie to Walden Pond and his haven there even more definitely by selling the cabin at Walden to Hugh Whelan, Emerson's gardener. That autumn, also, he took a little stock of himself when he finally answered an inquiry from the secretary of his Harvard Class of 1837—

"I don't know whether mine is a profession, or a trade, or what not. It is not yet learned, and in every instance has been practised before being studied. The mercantile part of it was begun *here* by myself alone.

"—It is not one but legion. I will give you some of the monster's heads. I am a Schoolmaster—a Private Tutor, a Surveyor—a Gardener, a Farmer—a Painter, I mean a House Painter, a Carpenter, a Mason, a Day-Laborer, a Pencil-Maker, a Glass-paper Maker, a Writer, and sometimes a Poetaster. If you will act the part of Iolas, and apply a hot iron to any of these heads, I shall be greatly obliged to you.

"My present employment is to answer such orders as may be expected from so general an advertisement as the above—that is, if I see fit, which is not always the case, for I have found out a way to live without what is commonly called employment or industry attractive or otherwise. Indeed my steadiest employment, if such it can be called, is to keep myself at the top of my condition, and ready for whatever may turn up in heaven or on earth. For the last two or three years I have lived in Concord woods alone, something more than a mile from any neighbor, in a house built entirely by myself."

He might have added that he had lived at Walden Pond for two years and two months at an average cost of twenty-seven cents a day. He did add in a postscript that if any members of the Class of 1837 "are in want of pecuniary assistance, and will make known their case to me, I will engage to give them some advice of more worth than money."

The resumption of his life at the Emerson house meant a renewal of his entertainment of the Emerson children and their guests, of the trivial cares of housekeeping and caring for the grounds. Though his journal contained little of his daily chores, the letters he wrote to Emerson in England did. "I have banked up the young trees against the winter and the mice, and I will look out, in my careless way, to see when a pale is loose or a nail drops out of its place. The broad gaps, at least, I will occupy. . . . The world is a cow that is hard to milk,—life does not come so easy,—and oh, how thinly it is watered ere we get it! . . .

"Lidian and I make very good housekeepers. She is a very dear sister to me. Ellen and Edith and Eddy and Aunty Brown keep up the tragedy and comedy and tragic-comedy of life as usual. . . . Eddy . . . occasionally surveys mankind from my shoulders as wisely as ever Johnson did. I respect him not a little, though it is I

77

that lift him up so unceremoniously. . . . He very seriously asked me, the other day, 'Mr. Thoreau, will you be my father?' I am occasionally Mr. Rough-and-tumble with him that I may not miss *him,* and lest he should miss *you* too much. So you must come back soon, or you will be superseded."

He wrote Emerson of the little affairs of Concord. "Mr. Hosmer has been working at a tannery in Stow for a fortnight, though he has just now come home sick. . . . Mrs. Hosmer remains here, and John looks stout enough to fill his own shoes and his father's too. . . . Mr. Blood and his company have at length seen the stars through the great telescope, and he told me he thought it was worth the while. . . ." And the affairs of Cambridge—"Cambridge college is really beginning to wake up and redeem its character and overtake the age. I see by the catalogue that they are about establishing a scientific school in connection with the university . . . Agassiz will erelong commence his lectures in the zoological department. A chemistry class has already been formed under the direction of Professor Horsford."

He informed Emerson, too, that he had had "a tragic correspondence, for the most part all on one side" with Miss Sophia Foord, who had not long since lived under the same roof, where she had tutored the young Emersons, though she had been gone over half a year when she had written to Thoreau, proposing that they be married. "She did really wish to—I hesitate to write—marry me. That is the way they spell it. Of course I did not write a deliberate answer. How could I deliberate upon it? I sent back as distinct a *no* as I have learned to pronounce after considerable practice, and I trust that this *no* has succeeded. Indeed, I wished that it might burst, like hollow shot, after it had struck and buried itself and made itself felt there. *There was no other way. I really had anticipated no such foe as this in my career."*

He wrote little of himself. "I do not know what to say of myself. I sit before my green desk, in the chamber at the head of the stairs, and attend to my thinking, sometimes more, sometimes less distinctly. I am not unwilling to think great thoughts if there are any in the wind, but what they are I am not sure. They suffice to keep me awake while the day lasts, at any rate. Perhaps they will redeem some portion of the night erelong."

He had "nothing worth writing" about his book. "Wiley & Putnam, Munroe, the Harpers, and Crosby & Nichols have all declined printing it with the least risk to themselves; but Wiley & Putnam will print it in their series, and any of them, anywhere, at *my* risk." Nevertheless, he was concerned about his book, though he wrote to Emerson that he was "indifferent." He was in the process of settling in his mind whether he should continue to hope for a publisher who might take on his book, or whether he should frankly arrange for its publication himself; it was a problem that touched less upon his vanity—that did not concern him at all—than it did upon the simple finances involved, since the sum required would not be one that could be worked up at twenty-seven cents a day.

He bent himself to do more lecturing. Late in January he delivered *The Rights and Duties of the Individual in Relation to Government*—the first public version of *Civil Disobedience*—to the Concord Lyceum. Requests to lecture outside Concord, however, were not easily come by, though before 1848 was done, he had such invitations, principally because Nathaniel Hawthorne persuaded the managers of the Salem Lyceum to ask Thoreau to lecture, which he did, on the economy of

79

student life in New England, in some part a portion of *Walden*.

In 1848, too, Horace Greeley managed to sell *Ktaadn and the Maine Woods*—for which he had paid Thoreau $25 himself—to the *Union Magazine* at three times that fee, part of which he sent Thoreau. Greeley had faithfully represented Thoreau, who was not a prolific writer and who was, from the point-of-view of an editor, not easy to deal with in his impatience and his desire to make constant changes in his manuscript and his objection to any editing.

Perhaps the most important event of 1848 for Thoreau was the opening of a correspondence of ideas with Harrison G. O. Blake, of Worcester, Massachusetts, a Harvard graduate, once a Unitarian minister, who had reread Thoreau's article on Aulus Persius Flaccus in *The Dial*, and had seen new depth and meaning in it. He wrote with the enthusiasm of a sycophant asking about the "significance" of Thoreau's life on the threshold of Thoreau's fourth decade. Late in March, 1848, Thoreau answered him.

"I do believe that the outward and the inward life correspond; that if any should succeed to live a higher life, others would not know of it; that difference and distance are one. To set about living a true life is to go a journey to a distant country, gradually to find ourselves surrounded by new scenes and men; and as long as the old are around me, I know that I am not in any true sense living a new or a better life. The outward is only the outside of that which is within. Men are not concealed under habits, but are revealed by them; they are their true clothes. . . .

"I do believe in simplicity. It is astonishing as well as sad, how many trivial affairs even the wisest man thinks he must attend to in a day; how singular an affair he thinks he must omit. When the mathematician would solve a difficult problem, he first frees the equation of all incumbrances, and reduces it to its simplest terms. So simplify the problem of life, distinguish the necessary and the real. Probe the earth to see where your main roots run. I would stand upon facts. . . .

"My actual life is a fact in view of which I have no occasion to congratulate myself, but for my faith and aspiration I have respect. It is from these that I speak. Every man's position is in fact too simple to be described. I have sworn no oath. I have no designs on society—or nature—or God. I am simply what I am, or I begin to be that. I *live* in the *present*. I only remember the past—and anticipate the future. I love to live, I love reform better than its modes. . . .

"If you would convince a man that he does wrong, do right. But do not care to convince him.—Men will believe what they see. Let them see.

"Pursue, keep up with, circle round and round your life as a dog does his master's chaise. Do what you love. Know your own bone; gnaw at it, bury it, unearth it, and gnaw it still. Do not be too moral. You may cheat yourself out of much life so. Aim above morality. Be not *simply* good—be good for something.—All fables indeed have their morals, but the innocent enjoy the story.

"Let nothing come between you and the light. Respect men as brothers only. When you travel to the celestial city, carry no letter of introduction. When you knock ask to see God—none of the servants. In what concerns you much do not think that you have companions—know that you are alone in the world."

Thus opened a correspondence which was to continue for the rest of Thoreau's life. For some time, while Blake

81

probed Thoreau, the tenor of their correspondence continued on this level of ideas; Blake manifestly wanted to know all he could about Thoreau. "If one hesitates in his path, let him not proceed," wrote Thoreau in his second letter to Blake, less than six weeks later. "Let him respect his doubts, for doubts, too, may have some divinity in them. That we have but little faith is not sad, but that we have but little faithfulness. By faithfulness faith is earned. When, in the progress of a life, a man swerves, though only by an angle infinitely small, from his proper and allotted path . . . then the drama of his life turns to tragedy, and makes haste to its fifth act. . . .

"I am of kin to the sod, and partake largely of its dull patience,—in winter expecting the sun of spring. In my cheapest moments I am apt to think that it is not my business to be 'seeking the spirit,' but as much its business to be seeking me. I know very well what Goethe meant when he said that he never had a chagrin but he made a poem out of it. I have altogether too much patience of this kind. I am too easily contented with a slight and almost animal happiness. My happiness is a good deal like that of the woodchucks.

"Methinks I am never quite committed, never wholly the creature of my moods, being always to some extent their critic. My only integral experience is in my vision. I see, perchance, with more integrity than I feel."

In July of 1848, Emerson returned from England, and Thoreau left the Emerson house to live once again with his family, resuming his endless walking and writing, and once more making pencils and surveying when called upon to do so, biding his time until the dream of book publication became the reality.

CHAPTER 6

Cape Cod and Concord

There is a sort of homely truth and naturalness in some books which is very rare to find, and yet looks cheap enough. There may be nothing lofty in the sentiment, or fine in the expression, but it is careless country talk. Homeliness is almost as great a merit in a book as in a house, if the reader would abide there. It is next to beauty, and a very high art. Some have this merit only. The scholar is not apt to make this most familiar experience come gracefully to the aid of his expression. Very few men can speak of Nature, for instance, with any truth. They overstep her modesty, somehow or other, and confer no favor. They do not speak a good word for her. Most cry better than they speak, and you get more nature out of them by pinching them than by addressing them. The surliness with which the wood-chopper speaks of his woods, handling them as indifferently as his axe, is better than the mealy-mouthed enthusiasm of the lover of Nature. Better that the primrose by the river's brim be a yellow primrose, and nothing more, than that it be something less. . . . But a good book will never have been forestalled, but the topic itself will in one sense be new, and its author, by consulting with Nature, will consult not only with those who have gone before, but with those who may come after. There is always room and occasion enough for a true book on any subject; as there is room for more light the brightest day and more rays will not interfere with the first.

—A WEEK ON THE CONCORD AND MERRIMACK RIVERS

By 1849, Thoreau was committed to the publication of *A Week on the Concord and Merrimack Rivers* at his own expense. He had had estimates from W. D. Ticknor & Company ("Say—1000 Cops. 448 pages like Emerson's Essays 1st series printed on good paper @ . . . $501.24") and from Munroe, also of Boston. It was to Munroe that the manuscript finally went early that year. Thoreau had committed himself to a financial obligation greater than any he had heretofore assumed.

His income to defray the costs he had agreed to pay for his new book did not materially increase. He lectured for a second time on his Walden experience in Salem in mid-February. A month later he lectured in Portland, Maine, on the same subject. His cousin, George Thatcher, asked him to address the Bangor Lyceum, since he was already in Maine and thus not far away; he quoted a fee of twenty-five dollars. Thoreau, however, was busy with the proofs of his book and did not want to go to Bangor for but one lecture, writing, "unless I should hear that they want *two* lectures to be read in *one* week or nearer together, I shall have to decline coming, this time." Thatcher was not able to arrange for two lectures and wrote Thoreau to this effect; his letter was waiting for Thoreau at Portland. Thoreau was not displeased; he had not wanted to go, having grown somewhat disenchanted with lecturing at relatively limited remuneration. "I am just in the midst of printing my book, which is likely to turn out much larger than I expected. I shall advertise another, 'Walden, or Life in the Woods,' in the first . . ." Presumably his second book was ready in manuscript by this time, though it was certainly not yet in its final form.

In April, Elizabeth Peabody asked him to retouch *Resistance to Civil Government* for use in a periodical she intended to publish occasionally. "I have so much writing to do at present," he wrote her, "with the printers in the rear of me, that I have almost no time left, but for bodily exercise; however, I will send you the article in question before the end of next week. If this will not be soon enough, will you please inform me by the next mail?" He added a postscript: "I offer the paper to your *first volume* only." *Resistance to Civil Government* appeared in the May issue of *Aesthetic Papers*—Miss Peabody's first, and, since public reception was disappointing, her only issue. Busy as he was, Thoreau went in mid-April to lecture at Worcester, the first of a series of lectures Harrison Blake obtained for him there; this lecture was followed by a second only a week later.

Late in May, James Munroe brought out *A Week on the Concord and Merrimack Rivers.* At the time of its publication, however, Thoreau was caught up in the slow dying of his older sister Helen. Her death occurred on the fourteenth of June. She had been declining in health through the winter and spring, and was the second of that congenial family circle to die. She was but 37, three years short of normal life expectancy for women in Massachusetts at that time. Though Thoreau's new book was in hand, she had very probably read the work in manuscript or had had it read to her by Thoreau himself. Thoreau's concern for her took precedence over the publication of his first book. He had written his cousin George Thatcher in February—taking the occasion of the Portland lecture to inquire about "statistics of a winter excursion to Chesuncook" in Maine—that he did not "wish to foresee what change may take place in her condition or in my own" in reference to Helen's "gradually failing" health.

After her death, he looked to his first book. Like every author, Thoreau was buoyed aloft by his hopes. Like every author, he expected to be acclaimed by reviewers and accepted by enough of the reading public to make a little money, not only through sales of the book, but through the increased demand for his lectures brought about by his mounting prestige as an author. Perhaps only the author who has passed through the fire of experience can look upon publication of a book with more tempered judgment. Only that author who has already had his hopes dashed has learned not to raise his hopes too high.

Copies of the book were sent to selected readers and critics in England, particularly to those who might be thought sympathetic. Copies for review went to the leading newspapers and magazines of the day, and, of course, to Thoreau's friends. Like all other authors, Thoreau could not believe that his friends, out of various motives, were apt to be his least reliable critics. Alcott's enthusiasm may have been balm to Thoreau. Alcott thought that the book would be "a popular book with our people here." Emerson thought it "fresh as the wild flag," and a beautiful book in the poetry of its descriptive passages.

Alcott's judgment, however sound in regard to the book's literary value, was wide of the mark insofar as public reception was concerned. In New York, Horace Greeley, anxious to do everything he could for Thoreau's book, assigned it for a feature review to George Ripley. The *New York Tribune* had a wide influence and Greeley hoped to carry word of Thoreau's abilities throughout its range. Unhappily, his choice of reviewer was not a good one for that purpose. Though Ripley thought *A Week on the Concord and Merrimack Rivers* "very near a fresh, original, thoughtful work," in which the "observations of Nature are as genial as Nature itself, and the tones" of Thoreau's "harp have an Aeolian sweetness," and while Thoreau's "reflections are always striking, often profoundly truthful, and his scholastic treasures, though a little too ostentatiously displayed, are such

86

as the best instructed reader will enjoy and thank him for," he was repelled by Thoreau's philosophy, "which is the Pantheistic egotism vaguely characterized as Transcendental." He said, "It seems second-hand, imitative, often exaggerated—a bad specimen of a dubious and dangerous school."

All this was set forth in the very first paragraph of the review. Many a reader of book reviews goes no farther than the first paragraph if he finds in it such disapproval that strikes a note of harmony in him. No matter what Ripley might write farther along in his review, he had done the book irreparable harm in his opening paragraph. He went on to quote liberally from the book after setting forth that Thoreau was "a scholar, a laborer, and in some sort a hermit" whose main purpose in life seemed to be "to demonstrate how slender an impediment is poverty to a man who pampers no superfluous wants, and how truly independent and self-sufficing is he who is in no manner the slave of his own appetites." But he inevitably returned to the attack on Thoreau's philosophy and charged him with an attack on the Bible. "Can that which Milton and Newton so profoundly reverenced . . . be wisely turned off by a youth . . . ? Mr. Thoreau's treatment of this subject seems revolting alike to good sense and good taste." Ripley concluded his review by inviting Thoreau to answer in his defense through the columns of the *Tribune,* but Thoreau had no taste for theologic controversy and made no reply to the review.

Ripley's review appeared within a month of publication—on June 13, 1849—and it unquestionably had an adverse effect on sales. But it did not alone slow sales of Thoreau's book. The fact remained that Thoreau's was as yet a new by-line on a book; at the same time it was true that his book was launched into a reading world which still held that practically all the worthwhile books written in English were written by British authors; and it could not be denied that the average reader who approached the book, invited by its title to a leisurely and pastoral journey along American waterways, was not prepared for Thoreau's philosophical digressions—the jewel-like essays which Thoreau had mined from his journal.

By the time James Russell Lowell's more favorable review appeared in *The Massachusetts Quarterly Review* for December, 1849, it was too late to do Thoreau's first venture between hardbound covers much good. Though not without criticism of the book, Lowell's review was on the whole a gratifying one. "It is like a book dug up, that has no date to assign it a special contemporaneousness, and no name of author. It has been written with no uncomfortable sense of a public looking over the shoulder. And the author is the least ingredient in it, too." If, in Lowell's opinion, Thoreau, "like most solitary men, exaggerates the importance of his own thoughts," it was also true for him that Thoreau's style was "compact and the language has an antique purity like wine grown colorless with age," and that the book "abounds in fine thoughts, and there is many a critical *obiter dictum* which is good law . . ."

By the time that Lowell's review appeared, it must have been brought home to Thoreau that his first book was a failure insofar as public acceptance and sales were concerned. It was comforting to be told by the English historian, J. A. Froude, in a letter from England, "In your book . . . I see hope for the coming world. . . . I wish to shake hands with you, and look a brave honest man in the face. In the mean time I will but congratulate you on the age in which your work is cast, the world has never seen one more pregnant."—but this praise from Britain was offset by condescending notices in British periodicals.

Thoreau spent no time mourning its failure. He went about his business in Concord, as always. He frequented the woods and the river, and from time to time went to Emerson's, not so much for intellectual stimulation as simply to befriend the children, as on one summer day when Ellen, now ten, was visiting her cousins at Staten Island, and Thoreau wrote her engagingly about his own visit at her home—"Eddy has got him a fish-pole and line with a pin-hook at the end, which he flourishes over the dry ground and the carpet at the risk of tearing out our eyes; but when I told him that he must have a cork and a sinker, his mother took off the pin and tied on a cork instead; but he doubts whether that will catch fish as well. He tells me that he is five years old. Indeed I was present at the celebration of his birthday lately, and supplied the company with onion and squash pipes, and rhubarb whistles, which is the most I can do on such occasions. Little Sammy Hoar blowed them most successfully, and made the loudest noise, though it almost strained his eyes out to do it. Edith is full of spirits. When she comes home from school, she goes hop skip and jump down into the field to pick berries, currants, gooseberries, raspberries, and thimbleberries; if there is one of these that has thoughts of changing its hue by to-morrow morning, I guess that Edith knows something about it and will consign it to her basket for Grandmamma."

That summer, too, Harrison Blake began to visit Thoreau—sometimes alone, sometimes with Theophilus Brown, a Worcester tailor, and they accompanied Thoreau on his excursions into the woods. On at least one occasion they discussed Thoreau's book, which Blake liked, and later Thoreau wrote him, "I thank you for your hearty appreciation of my book. I am glad to have had such a long talk with you, and that you had patience to listen to me to the end. I think that I have the advantage of you, for I chose my own mood, and in one sense your mood too, that is a quiet and attentive reading mood."

In October, 1849, Thoreau set out on a trip to Cape Cod with Ellery Channing. They went by way of Cohasset, where a hundred forty-five lives had been lost, impelled by curiosity. The lost lives were principally Irish immigrants. "We found many Irish in the cars, going to identify bodies and to sympathize with the survivors and also to attend the funeral which was to take place in the afternoon . . ." His first sight of the coast was at the scene of the tragedy—"said to be the rockiest shore in Massachusetts,—from Nantasket to Scituate,—hard sienitic rocks, which the waves have laid bare, but have not been able to crumble.

"The brig St. John, from Galway, Ireland, laden with emigrants, was wrecked on Sunday morning; it was now Tuesday morning, and the sea was still breaking violently on the rocks. There were eighteen or twenty . . . large boxes . . . lying on a green hillside, a few rods from the water, and surrounded by a crowd. The bodies which had been recovered, twenty-seven or eight in all, had been collected there." The scene did not make the impression on Thoreau he had thought it would. "If I had found one body cast upon the beach in some lonely place, it would have affected me more. . . . If the last day were come, we should not think so much about the separation of friends or the blighted prospects of individuals."

Thoreau carried with him the eighth volume of the

Collections of the Massachusetts Historical Society, containing information about the Cape towns, and used it for reference. Undoubtedly he intended to use his excursion in his lectures; the journey to Maine had earned him some money in subsequent lectures; there was reason to suppose that Cape Cod would make as interesting a subject. His account, however, was more that of the traveler than of the naturalist, but very often there was a pleasant combination of the views.

"The windmills on the hills,—large weather-stained octagonal structures,—and the salt-works scattered all along the shore, with their long rows of vats resting on piles driven into the marsh, their low, turtle-like roofs, and their slighter windmills, were novel and interesting objects to an inlander. The sand by the roadside was partially covered with bunches of a moss-like plant, *Hudsonia tomentosa*, which a woman in the stage told us was called 'poverty-grass,' because it grew where nothing else would."

Among the common people of the Cape Thoreau was thoroughly at home, as he was with Therien, the woodchopper, and Hugh Quoil the Irishman, and the Hosmers and others of his townsmen who lived close to the land and pretended to no eminence of mind or material possessions. "I was struck by the pleasant equality which reigned among the stage company, and their broad and invulnerable good humor. They were what is called free and easy, and met one another to advantage, as men who had, at length, learned how to live. They appeared to know each other when they were strangers, they were so simple and downright. They were well met, in an unusual sense, that is, they met as well as they could meet, and did not seem to be troubled with any impediment. . . . It was evident that the same foolish respect was not here claimed for mere wealth and station that is in many parts of New England; yet some of them were the 'first people,' as they were called, of the various towns through which we passed. Retired sea-captains, in easy circumstances, who talked of farming as sea-captains are wont; an erect, respectable, and trustworthy-looking man, in his wrapper, some of the salt of the earth, who had formerly been the salt of the sea; or a more courtly gentleman, who, perchance, had been a representative to the General Court in his day; or a broad, red-faced Cape Cod man, who had seen too many storms to be easily irritated; or a fisherman's wife, who had been waiting a week for the coaster to leave Boston, and had at length come by the cars.

"A strict regard for truth obliges us to say, that the few women whom we saw that day looked exceedingly pinched up. They had prominent chins and noses, having lost all their teeth, and a sharp W would represent their profile. They were not so well preserved as their husbands; or perchance they were well preserved as dried specimens. (Their husbands, however, were pickled.) . . ." He added to this note a whimsical aside about his "own dental system" being "far from perfect,"—and two years later had false teeth.

Thoreau noted the dwarfed apple trees ("One, which had been set ten years, was on an average eighteen inches high, and spread nine feet, with a flat top. It had borne one bushel of apples two years before."), the strangeness of the Cape landscape ("to an inlander . . . a constant mirage"), the prevailing "crops" ("The shores are more fertile than the dry land. The inhabitants measure their crops, not only by bushels of corn, but by barrels of clams. A thousand barrels of clam-bait are counted as equal in value to six or eight thousand bushels of Indian corn . . ."), the emetic quality of clams ("In the course of the evening I began to feel the potency of the clam which I had eaten, and I was obliged to confess to our host that I was no tougher than the cat he told me of . . . and I was made quite sick by it for a short time, while he laughed at my expense.").

On the third day of their excursion, they came to the beach beyond the Nauset Lights on the way to Province-town; it brought out again the poet in Thoreau. "The white breakers were rushing to the shore; the foam ran up the sand, and then ran back, as far as we could see (and we imagined how much farther along the Atlantic coast, before and behind us), as regularly, to compare great things with small, as the master of a choir beats time with his white wand; and ever and anon a higher wave caused us hastily to deviate from our path, and we looked back on our tracks filled with water and foam. The breakers looked like droves of a thousand wild horses of Neptune, rushing to the shore, with their white manes streaming far behind; and when, at length, the sun shone for a moment, their manes were rainbow-tinted. Also, the long kelp-weed was tossed up from time to time, like the tails of sea-cows sporting in the brine.

"There was not a sail in sight . . . and the only human beings whom we saw on the beach for several days were one or two wreckers looking for driftwood . . . We soon met one of these wreckers,—a regular Cape Cod man, with whom we parleyed, with a bleached and weather-beaten face, within whose wrinkles I distinguished no particular feature. It was like an old sail endowed with life,—a hanging-cliff of weather-beaten flesh,—like one of the clay boulders which occurred in that sand-bank. . . . He looked as if he sometimes saw a doughnut, but never descended to comfort; too grave to laugh, too tough to cry; as indifferent as a clam,—like a sea-clam with hat on and legs, that was out walking the strand. He may have been one of the Pilgrims,—Peregrine White, at least,—who has kept on the back side of the Cape, and let the centuries go by."

They roamed the Cape for a week and then turned back to Concord. "When we reached Boston . . . , I had a gill of Provincetown sand in my shoes, and at Concord there was still enough left to sand my pages for many a day . . ."—and enough material for a lecture or two.

By 1850, Thoreau had resigned himself to the failure of *A Week on the Concord and Merrimack Rivers.* Nothing of the book appeared in his letters or the entries in his journal. He wrote long letters to Harrison Blake, still absorbed in philosophical matters, sometimes with theological references—("Let God alone if need be. Methinks, if I loved him more, I should keep him,—I should keep myself rather,—at a more respectful distance. It is not when I am going to meet him, but when I am just turning away and leaving him alone, that I discover that God is.")—and he wrote a pungent note of advice about conforming—("As for conforming outwardly, and living your own life inwardly, I do not think much of that.")—as well as some preaching ("Drink deep or taste not of the Pierian spring. Be not deterred by melancholy on the path which leads to immortal health & joy. When they tasted of the water of the river which they were to go, they thought that tasted a little bitterish to the palate, but it proved sweeter when it was down.").

That year the Thoreau family left the Texas house and moved into the Yellow House on the Main Street of Concord, Thoreau's final home. For a brief time that May Thoreau had a surveying job in Haverhill, found for him by his cousin Charles Dunbar, but he was back in Concord by the end of May. And in July Emerson called upon him to discharge a melancholy commission; Emerson had learned that their mutual friend Margaret Fuller—now Margaret Ossoli, she having married in Italy —had drowned at Fire Island in the wrecking of the ship bearing the Ossoli family home; he asked Thoreau to go at once to Fire Island and salvage any of her property that could be found. Thoreau went, but reached the scene five days after the accident, and found little to recover. He did not linger at the scene any longer than he needed to—five days—returning home virtually empty-handed. Scarcely a fortnight later he wrote of the event to Blake—

"I find that actual events, notwithstanding the singular prominence which we all allow them, are far less real than the creations of my imagination. They are truly visionary and insignificant,—all that we commonly call life and death,—and affect me less than my dreams. This petty stream which from time to time swells and carries away the mills and bridges of our habitual life, and that mightier stream or ocean on which we securely float,— what makes the difference between them? I have in my pocket a button which I ripped off the coat of the Marquis of Ossoli, on the seashore, the other day. Held up, it intercepts the light,—an actual button,—and yet all the life it is connected with is less substantial to me, and interests me less, than my faintest dream. Our thoughts are the epochs in our lives: all else is but as a journal of the winds that blew while we were here."

He developed this theme at greater length in his journal. He was once again making many entries in his journal, including paragraphs which he added to the manuscript of *Walden,* that second book he still dreamed of seeing in print, and which he revised from time to time. Between periods of employment as a surveyor—employment which he performed with highly satisfactory precision—he continued his solitary walks, striving, as always, to avoid people who might take his precious time with small talk he did not want to hear.

Concord by this time had learned to accept him for what he was. There might still be those who scorned him as a loafer, but, after all, he did help make pencils, he was the local surveyor, and he went about lecturing—for money. Undoubtedly his walks and his attitudes made him a local "character," which he was already on the way to becoming when, some years before, Dr. Ripley had dubbed Thoreau and his walking companions the third church in Concord—the Walden Pond Association.

Gone from the journal now and thereafter were the multiple quotations from what Thoreau read—and he did still read, having only late in 1849 persuaded President Jared Sparks of Harvard to permit him to take books from the Harvard Library ("I ask only that the University may help to finish the education, whose foundations she has helped to lay. I was not then ripe for her higher courses, and now that I am riper I trust that I am not too far away to be instructed by her."). His observation now was sharper, and his appreciation of his native countryside went deeper.

"In all my rambles I have seen no landscape which can make me forget Fair Haven. I still sit on its Cliff in a new spring day, and look over the awakening woods and the river, and hear the new birds sing, with the same delight as ever. It is as sweet a mystery to me as ever, what this world is. Fair Haven Lake in the south, with its pine-covered island and its meadows, the hickories putting out fresh young yellowish leaves, and the oaks light-grayish ones, while the oven-bird thrums his sawyer-like strain, and the chewink rustles through the dry leaves or repeats his jingle on a tree-top, and the wood thrush, the genius of the wood, whistles for the first time his clear and thrilling strain,—it sounds as it did the first time I heard it. The sight of these budding woods intoxicates me . . .

"The life in us is like the water in the river; it may rise this year higher than ever it was known to before and flood the uplands—even this may be the eventful year—and drown out all our muskrats.

"There are as many strata at different levels of life as there are leaves in a book. Most men probably have lived in two or three. When on the higher levels we can remember the lower levels, but when on the lower we cannot remember the higher.

"My imagination, my love and reverence and admiration, my sense of the miraculous, is not so excited by any event as by the remembrance of my youth. Men talk about Bible miracles because there is no miracle in their lives. Cease to gnaw that crust. There is ripe fruit over your head. . . .

"My friends wonder that I love to walk alone in solitary fields and woods by night. Sometimes in my loneliest and wildest midnight walk I hear the sound of the whistle and the rattle of the cars, where perchance some of those very friends are being whirled by night over, as they think, a well-known, safe, and public road. I see that men do not make or choose their own paths whether they are railroads or trackless through the wilds, but what the powers permit each one enjoys. My solitary course has the same sanction that the Fitchburg Railroad has. If they have a charter from Massachusetts and—what is of much more importance—from Heaven, to travel the course and in the fashion they do, I have a charter, though it be from

Heaven alone, to travel the course I do,—to take the necessary lands and pay the damages. It is by the grace of God in both cases. . . ."

He was traveling ever more widely in Concord, expanding his range in his own corner of the earth.

CHAPTER 7

Action from Principle

> *However mean your life is, meet it and live; do not shun it and call it hard names. It is not so bad as you are. It looks poorest when you are richest. The fault-finder will find faults even in paradise. Love your life, poor as it is. You may perchance have some pleasant, thrilling, glorious hours, even in a poorhouse. The setting sun is reflected from the windows of the almshouse as brightly as from the rich man's house. The snow melts before its door as early in the spring. I do not see but a quiet mind may live as contentedly there, and have as cheering thoughts as anywhere, and, indeed, the town's poor seem to live the most independent lives of any. They are simply great enough to receive without misgiving. Cultivate poverty like sage, like a garden herb. Do not trouble yourself to get new things, whether clothes or friends. That is dissipation. Turn the old; return to them. Things do not change; we change. If I were confined to a corner in a garret all my days, like a spider, the world would be just as large to me while I had my thoughts.* —JOURNAL, 1850

IN September, 1850, wanting "one honest walk" in Canada, Thoreau set out with Ellery Channing on an inexpensive journey to Montreal and Quebec. He carried the baggage he took wrapped in paper, and meant to rough it. They went by train.

Thoreau had not traveled far in Quebec before he was aware of the inadequacy of his clothing. "It already looked and felt a good deal colder than it had in New England, and we might have expected it would. I realized fully that I was four degrees nearer the pole, and shuddered at the thought . . . It was an atmosphere that made me think of the fur-trade, which is so interesting a department in Canada, for I had for all head-covering a thin palm-leaf hat without lining, that cost twenty-five cents, and over my coat one of those unspeakably cheap, as well as thin, brown linen sacks of the Oak Hall pattern, which every summer appear all over New England, thick as the leaves upon the trees. It was a thoroughly Yankee costume, which some of my fellow-travelers wore in the cars to save their coats a dusting. . . . I never wear my best coat on a journey, though perchance I could show a certificate to prove that I have a more costly one, at least, at home, if that were all that a gentleman required. . . . Honest traveling is about as dirty work as you can do, and a man needs a pair of over-alls for it. As for blacking my shoes in such a case, I should as soon think of blacking my face. I carry a piece of tallow to preserve the leather and keep out the water; that's all; and many an officious shoe-black, who carried off my shoes when I was slumbering, mistaking me for a gentleman, has had occasion to repent it before he produced a gloss on them."

Along the heights at Quebec he and Channing walked, plucking flowers. "There was an abundance of succory still in blossom, broad-leaved goldenrod, buttercups, thorn bushes, Canada thistles, and ivy, on the very summit of Cape Diamond. I also found the bladder campion . . ." They walked to the Falls of St. Anne, thirty miles away, self-styled the "Knights of the Umbrella and the Bundle," Thoreau keeping notes, which as often as not drew upon what earlier travelers had written of the St. Lawrence and its environs. To Thoreau, Canada appeared "as old as Normandy itself, and realized much that I had heard of Europe and the Middle Ages. Even the names of humble Canadian villages affected me as if they had been those of the renowned cities of antiquity. To be told by a habitant, when I asked the name of a village in sight, that it is *St. Feréol* or *St. Anne,* the *Guardian Angel* or the *Holy Joseph's;* or of a mountain, that it was *Bélange* or *St. Hyacinthe!* As soon as you leave the States, these saintly names begin. *St. Johns* is the first town you stop at . . . , and thence-forward, the names of the mountains, and streams, and villages reel, if I may so speak, with the intoxication of poetry,—*Chambly, Longueuil, Pointe aux Trembles, Bartholomy,* etc., etc.; as if it needed only a little foreign accent, a few more liquids and vowels perchance in the language, to make us locate our ideals at once. I began to dream of Provence and the Troubadours, and of places and things which have no existence on the earth. They veiled the Indian and the primitive forest, and the woods toward Hudson's Bay were only as the forests of France and Germany. I could not at once bring myself to believe that the inhabitants who pronounced daily those beautiful and, to me, significant names lead as prosaic lives as we of New England. In short, the Canada which I saw was not merely a place for railroads to terminate in and for criminals to run to."

They visited waterfalls ("It was evident that this was the country for waterfalls; that every stream that empties into the St. Lawrence, for some hundreds of miles, must have a great fall or cascade on it . . ."), fortifications ("The most modern fortifications have an air of antiquity about them; they have the aspect of ruins in better or worse repair from the day they are built, because they are not really the work of this age. The very place where the soldier resides has a peculiar tendency to become old and dilapidated, as the word *barrack* implies. I couple all fortifications in my mind with the dismantled Spanish forts to be found in so many parts of the world; and if in any place they are not actually dismantled, it is because that there the intellect of the inhabitants is dismantled. The commanding officer of an old fort near Valdivia in South America, when a traveler remarked to him that, with one discharge, his gun-carriages would certainly fall to pieces, gravely replied, 'No, I am sure, sir, they would stand two.' Perhaps the guns of Quebec would stand three."), and observed that the churches in Canada were magnificent in contrast to the houses. "The churches were very picturesque, and their interior much more showy than the dwelling-houses promised. They were of stone, for it was ordered, in 1699, that that should be their material. They had tinned spires, and quaint ornaments. . . . In Beauport . . . we turned aside to look at a church which was just being completed,—a very large and handsome edifice of stone, with a green bough stuck in its gable, . . . The comparative wealth of the Church in this country was apparent; for in this village we did not see one good house besides. They were all humble cottages; and yet this appeared to me a more imposing structure than any church in Boston."

They sampled Canadian fruit ("They said they had three kinds of plums growing wild,—blue, white, and red, the two former much alike and the best. Also they asked me if I would have . . . some apples, and got me some. They were exceedingly fair and glossy, and it was evident

102

that there was no worm in them; but they were as hard almost as a stone, as if the season was too short to mellow them."), remarked the insularity of the average Canadian's way of living ("Every New England house . . . has a front and principal door opening to the great world . . . but the Canadian's door opens into his backyard and farm alone, and the road which runs behind his house leads only from the church of one saint to that of another."), and viewed the scenery at Quebec with a critical eye ("Too much has not been said about the scenery of Quebec. The fortifications of Cape Diamond are omnipresent. They preside, they frown over the river and surrounding country. You travel ten, twenty, thirty miles up or down the river's banks, you ramble fifteen miles amid the hills on either side, and then, when you have long since forgotten them, perchance slept on them by the way, at a turn of the road or of your body, there they are still, with their geometry against the sky. . . . I associate the beauty of Quebec with the steel-like and flashing air, which may be peculiar to that season of the year . . .").

In a week the "honest walk" was done. Thoreau was back in Concord. He had traveled eleven hundred miles, at a total cost of $12.75. He would still, he recorded, like "right well to make a longer excursion on foot through the wilder parts of Canada." To tell the truth, he had not seen very much of Canada, he had barely covered a small portion of its inhabited surface, and his observations did not match those he had made in Maine or on Cape Cod, to say nothing of the continuing observations of his native place.

He was aware of the fleetness of his visit, for when his townsmen expected him to lecture on the subject "because I had *visited* it," he reflected that he had "visited it as the bullet visits the wall at which it is fired, and from which it rebounds as quickly. . . ." His explorations of Concord were in depth. He continued them, resuming his habits and his way of life, and demonstrating that no matter how many times a man walked a familiar path he might learn something new with each walk.

He sampled the wild apples. "I pluck them . . . fruit of old trees that have been dying ever since I was a boy and are not yet dead. . . . Frequented only by the wood-pecker, deserted now by the farmer, who has not faith enough to look under the boughs. Food for walkers. Sometimes apples red inside, perfused with a beautiful blush, faery food, too beautiful to eat,—apple of the evening sky, of the Hesperides. . . . The apples are now thawed. . . . Those which a month ago were sour, crabbed, and uneatable are now filled with a rich, sweet cider which I am better acquainted with than with wine. . . . Let the frost come to freeze them first solid as stones, and then the sun or a warm winter day—for it takes but little heat—to thaw them, and they will seem to have bor-rowed a flavor from heaven through the medium of the air in which they hang."

He went one evening to visit an Indian encampment and pursued his interests in their ways of living. He learned about hunting moose and caribou, how to use moose horns, how to imitate the sounds of moose and deer, how to cure the skin of these animals. He put into his journal crude drawings of their spears and traps. He added to his store of Indian lore because he hoped some day to write a book about the Indians. "Did not know use of eye in axe," he wrote in his journal. "Put a string through it and wore it round neck."

The year turned. On January 1, 1851, Thoreau lec-tured in Clinton on the subject of Cape Cod. While he was there, he visited the gingham-mills and set down in his journals the details of weaving. "I am struck by the fact that no work has been shirked when a piece of cloth is produced. Every thread has been counted in the finest web; it has not been matted together. The operator has succeeded only by patience, perseverance, and fidelity."

Later in the month he again lectured on his life at Walden, this time at Medford, and in May he spoke in Worcester once more on *Walking*. The day after his Worcester lecture he walked to Asnebumskit Hill in Paxton because it was said to be the highest land in Worcester County, next to Wachusett. "A very extensive view, but the western view not so much wilder as I expected. See Barre, about fifteen miles off, and Rutland, etc., etc. Not so much forest as in our neighborhood; high, swelling hills, but less shade for the walker."

In April of that year Thoreau, who had never been an Abolitionist, no matter how much he was opposed to slavery, was upset when Thomas Sims, a Negro living in Boston, was seized and sent back into slavery. He thought the Fugitive Slave Law monstrous cruelty and Massachusetts' adherence to it shameful. He took a crumb of comfort in the fact that Daniel Foster of Concord stood at the wharf as the Negro was taken away and read a prayer. "I could not help feeling a slight degree of pride because, of all the towns in the Commonwealth, Concord was the only one distinctly named as being represented in that new tea-party."

He held forth at length in his journal, expressing his convictions. "I wish my townsmen to consider that, whatever the human law may be, neither an individual nor a nation can ever deliberately commit the least act of injustice without having to pay the penalty for it. . . . I hear a good deal said about trampling this law under foot. Why, one need not go out of his way to do that. This law lies not at the level of the head or the reason. Its natural habitat is in the dirt. It was bred and has its life only in the dust and mire, on a level with the feet; and he who walks with freedom, unless, with a sort of quibbling and Hindoo mercy, he avoids treading on every venomous reptile, will inevitably tread on it, and so trample it under foot.

"It has come to this, that the friends of liberty, the friends of the slave, have shuddered when they have understood that his fate has been left to the legal tribunals, so-called, of the country to be decided. The people have no faith that justice will be awarded in such a case. . . . I would much rather trust to the sentiment of the people, which would itself be a precedent to posterity. . . .

"I think that recent events will be valuable as a criticism on the administration of justice in our midst, or rather as revealing what are the true sources of justice in any community. It is to some extent fatal to the courts when the people are compelled to go behind the courts. . . . As for measures to be adopted, among others I would advise abolitionists to make as earnest and vigorous and persevering assault on the press, as they have already made, and with effect too, on the church." Somewhat cautiously, he admitted that he did not believe "that the North will soon come to blows with the South on this question."—but he was manifestly not averse to the idea of war, for he added, "It would be too bright a page to be written in the history of the race at present."

He expressed his disgust and fury with the press, the editors of which, he maintained, supported the Fugitive Slave Law solely to "secure the approbation of their patrons, and also, one would think, because they are not aware that a sounder sentiment prevails to any extent." He fulminated for a month, pondering a talk on the subject, for which his jottings in the journal were notes.

The household abounded with Abolitionists. His late sister Helen had been an ardent Abolitionist; so were Mrs. Ward and Aunt Maria. They read Garrison's paper, *The Liberator;* so did Thoreau, who excepted it from his general condemnation of the press in the matter of slavery. But Thoreau did not belong to any of the abolitionist societies. He had a pronounced aversion to "reform" of people. But he lent a hand to aid fugitive slaves escape to Canada more than once, and the next time, after the Sims case, that the opportunity afforded itself, Thoreau did not hesitate to do what he could.

The occasion was the following October, on the first day of which at "5 P.M." he "put a fugitive slave, who has taken the name of Henry Williams, into the cars for Canada. He escaped from Stafford County, Virginia, to Boston last October; has been in Shadrach's place at the Cornhill Coffee-House; had been corresponding through an agent with his master, who is his father, about buying himself, his master asking $600, but he having been able to raise only $500. Heard that there were writs out for two Williamses, fugitives, and was informed by his fellow-servants and employer that Augerhole Burns and others of the police had called for him when he was out. Accordingly fled to Concord last night on foot, bringing a letter to our family from Mr. Lovejoy of Cambridge and another which Garrison had formerly given him on another occasion. He lodged with us, and waited in the house till funds were collected with which to forward him. Intended to dispatch him at noon through to Burlington, but when I went to buy his ticket, saw one at the depot who looked and behaved so much like a Boston policeman that I did not venture that time. An intelligent and very well-behaved man, a mulatto. . . .

"The slave said he could guide himself by many other stars than the north star, whose rising and setting he knew. They steered for the north star even when it had got round and appeared to them to be in the south. They frequently followed the telegraph when there was no railroad. The slaves bring many superstitions from Africa. The fugitives sometimes superstitiously carry a turf in their hats, thinking that their success depends on it."

But essentially slavery—and indeed all the concerns of his fellowmen—were secondary issues with Thoreau. His primary interest continued to be in the place he found himself, his native place, in men only insofar as they lived in the same place, especially those close to the land, like Therien and George Minott, and in aspects of nature seen and studied from time to time; he wrote about cobwebs, muskrat houses ("They have reduced life to a lower scale than Diogenes."), acorns, witchhazel ("an extremely interesting plant. . . . Its blossoms smell like the spring, like the willow catkins; by their color as well as fragrance they belong to the saffron dawn of the year, suggesting amid all these signs of autumn, falling leaves and frost, that the life of Nature, by which she eternally flourishes, is untouched."), the hooting of owls, new-fallen leaves, a moonlight walk ("It is as if you were walking in night up to your chin."), and little Johnny Riordan, the child of Irish parents left behind by the building of the Fitchburg Railroad ("They showed me Johnny Riordan today, with one thickness of ragged cloth over his little shirt for all this cold weather, with shoes with large holes in the toes, into which the snow got, as he said, without an outer garment, to walk a mile to school every day over the bleakest of causeways,—the clothes with countless patches, which hailed from, claimed descent from, were originally identical with, pantaloons of mine, which set as if his mother had fitted them to a tea-kettle first. This little mass of humanity, this tender gobbet for the fates, cast into a cold world with a torn lichen leaf wrapped about him,—Oh, I should rather hear that America's first-born were all slain than that his little fingers and toes should feel cold while I am warm. Is man so cheap that he cannot be clothed but with a mat, a rag, that we should bestow on him our *cold* victuals? Are there any fellow-creatures to whom we abandon our rags, to whom we give our old clothes and shoes when they will not fend the weather from ourselves? Let the mature rich wear the rags and insufficient clothing; let the infant poor wear the purple and fine linen. I shudder when I think of the fate of innocency. Our charitable institutions are an insult to humanity. A charity which dispenses the crumbs that fall from its overloaded tables, which are left after its feasts!'').

And in the middle of the following April Thoreau had one of those adventures in nature which were events in his days. Rounding the corner of Hubbard's Grove, he happened upon the first woodchuck of the season, and proceeded to make its acquaintance. "I ran along the fence and cut him off, or rather overtook him, though he started at the same time. When I was only a rod and a half off, he stopped, and I did the same; then he ran again, and I ran up within three feet of him, when he stopped again, the fence being between us. I squatted down and surveyed him at my leisure. His eyes were dull black and rather inobvious, with a faint chestnut (?) iris, with but little expression and that more of resignation than of anger. The general aspect was a coarse grayish brown, a sort of grisel (?). A lighter brown next the skin, then black or very dark brown and tipped with whitish rather loosely. The head between a squirrel and a bear, flat on the top and dark brown . . ."

He cornered the woodchuck, touched it with a stick, tried to open its gritting jaws with the stick. He got up next to it. "We sat looking at one another about half an hour, till we began to feel mesmeric influences. . . . He would not stir as long as I was looking at him or could see him. . . . I sat down by his side within a foot. I talked to him *quasi* forest lingo, baby-talk, at any rate in a conciliatory tone, and thought I had some influence on him. . . . With a little stick I lifted one of his paws to examine it, and held it up at pleasure. I turned him over to see what color he was beneath . . . I laid my hand on him. If I had had some food, I could have ended with stroking him at my leisure. . . . I respect him as one of the natives." Such intimate encounters added a dimension to his existence.

In February, 1852, he lectured in Plymouth, but he was evidently not as much interested in his audience or their reaction as he was in the evergreen winterberry and the descendants of the Pilgrims still alive in that town, and on the next day he was back on the railroad near Walden Pond "reminded of spring by the quality of the air. The cock-crowing and even the telegraph harp prophesy it . . ." He also lectured in Lincoln, but lecturing did not loom large in his journal, which he filled from day to day with sensitive entries about life in and around Concord.

Horace Greeley, still hoping to bring Thoreau to the attention of a wider audience than he had, wrote him that while he was not well enough known to lecture successfully in New York, he was yet "a better speaker than many, but a far better writer still," and proposed that

110

perhaps Thoreau might "swap" some of his "woodnotes wild" for "dollars." He urged him to write articles Greeley might sell for him.

Thoreau responded by sending him some articles—*The Iron Horse* and *A Poet Buying a Farm*—and proposing to send his account of the Canadian excursion. Within a month, Greeley had placed the two articles with *Sartain's Union Magazine* "for a low price," and had a letter from John Sartain, the editor, setting forth that "Mr. T. might send us some further contributions, and shall at least receive prompt and courteous decision respecting them." Greeley, however, was a little dubious about such a long article on Canada as Thoreau proposed and suggested that Thoreau break it up into three or four parts.

Once more Greeley proposed that Thoreau write an article on Emerson, a review of the man and his work— "Let it be calm, searching, and impartial; nothing like adulation, but a just summing up of what he is and what he has done." He was certain that he could find a place for this in the *Westminster Review,* and would pay Thoreau $50 for it—in advance, if Thoreau wished it. Thoreau did not wish it. Thoreau did not want to write about Emerson at all, still holding that it would be a presumption upon their friendship for him to do so.

Thoreau sent in his account of the Canadian trip—*A Yankee in Canada*. It was accepted by his old friend, George W. Curtis, editor of *Putnam's Magazine,* to be run in five instalments early in 1853. Curtis was also interested in seeing *Cape Cod,* and Thoreau sent him the first hundred pages later in the year. But Thoreau was unfortunate in his relations with *Putnam's*—friend or not, Curtis took it upon himself to censor Thoreau's manuscript and rid it of what Greeley called Thoreau's "defiant Pantheism."

111

Thoreau was outraged by the censoring of his work. He wrote Greeley, "I am sorry that my manuscript should be so mangled, insignificant as it is, but I do not know how I could have helped it fairly, since I was born to be a pantheist—if that be the name of me, and I do the deeds of one." He withdrew the final two chapters of *A Yankee in Canada* from *Putnam's*.

Though he considered his profession that of lecturing, and his employment, apart from making pencils on occasion, surveying, he was now writing more than ever. His entries in his journal for 1852 filled 750 pages. Nor was he alone concerned with nature in Concord, though he kept his townsmen out of his journal except for his recurring notes about the Irish and the trappers, muskrat-hunters, and woodsmen he encountered. Yet he was acquainted with the events of life in Concord, and viewed them with an amused detachment.

He wrote to Sophia that "Mr. Pierce the presidential candidate was in town . . . visiting Hawthorne whose college chum he was, and . . . Hawthorne is writing a life of him for electioneering purposes." He added, "Concord is just as idiotic as ever in relation to the spirits and their knockings. Most people here believe in a spiritual world which no respectable junk bottle which had not met with a slip—would condescend to contain even a portion of for a moment . . .—in spirits which the very bull frogs in our meadows would blackball. . . . The hooting of owls—the croaking of frogs—is celestial wisdom in comparison."

He continued to live very much in the bosom of his family, for all his wandering abroad. He enjoyed their company, if he sometimes vexed them. "My Aunt Maria," he wrote in his journal March 28, 1853, "asked me to read the life of Dr. Chalmers, which, however, I did not promise to do. Yesterday, Sunday, she was heard through the partition shouting to my Aunt Jane, who is deaf, 'Think of it! He stood half an hour to-day to hear the frogs croak, and he wouldn't read the life of Chalmers.' "

In that same month he was asked to fill out a blank for possible membership in the Association for the Advancement of Science. He was somewhat amused and wrote, "Now, though I could state to a select few that department of human inquiry which engages me, and should be rejoiced at an opportunity to do so, I felt that it would be to make myself the laughing-stock of the scientific community to describe or attempt to describe to them that branch of science which specially interests me, inasmuch as they do not believe in a science which deals with the higher law. . . . The fact is I am a mystic, a transcendentalist, and a natural philosopher to boot. . . . How absurd that, though I probably stand as near to nature as any of them, and am by constitution as good an observer as most, yet a true account of my relation to nature should excite their ridicule only! If it had been the secretary of an association of which Plato or Aristotle was the president, I should not have hesitated to describe my studies at once and particularly." Nevertheless, later in the year he did specify on the blank as a branch of science in which he felt especial interest "The Manners & Customs of the Indians of the Algonquin Group previous to contact with the civilized man."

He was considerably less loath to answer inquiries about his attitudes sent him by Harrison Blake early that year. "As to whether what you speak of as the 'world's way' (Which for the most part is my way) or that which is shown me, is the better, the former is imposture, the latter is truth. I have the coldest confidence in the last. . . . My hours are not 'cheap in such a way that *I* doubt

113

whether the world's way would not have been better,' but cheap in such a way, that I doubt whether the world's way, which I have adopted for the time, could be worse. The whole enterprise of this nation which is not an upward, but a westward one, toward Oregon, California, Japan &c, is totally devoid of interest to me, whether performed on foot or by a Pacific railroad. . . .

"As it respects these things I have not changed an opinion one iota from the first. As the stars looked to me when I was a shepherd in Assyria, they look to me now a New Englander. The higher the *mt.* on which you stand, the less change in the prospect from year to year, from age to age. . . . I have had but one *spiritual* birth . . . , and now whether it rains or snows, whether I laugh or cry, fall farther below or approach nearer my standard, whether Pierce or Scott is elected—not a new scintillation of light flashes on me, but ever and anon, though with longer intervals, the same surprising & everlastingly new light dawns to me, with only such variations as in the coming of the natural day, with which indeed, it is often coincident. . . .

"I very rarely indeed, if ever, 'feel any itching to be what is called useful to my fellowmen.' . . . What a foul subject is this, of doing good, instead of minding ones life, which should be his business. . . . Instead of taking care to flourish & smell & taste sweet and refresh all mankind to the extent of our capacity & quality. People will sometimes try to persuade you that you have done something from that motive, as if you did not already know enough about it. If I ever *did* a man any good, in their sense, of course it was something exceptional, and insignificant compared with the good or evil which I am constantly doing by being what I am. . . .

114

"The problem of life becomes one cannot say by how many degrees more complicated as our material wealth is increased . . . since the problem is not merely nor mainly to get life for our bodies, but by this or a similar discipline to get life for our souls . . . If I accomplish as much more in spiritual work as I am richer in worldly goods, then I am just as worthy, or worth just as much as I was before, and no more. I see that, in my own case, money *might* be of great service to me, but probably it would not be, for the difficulty ever is that I do not improve my opportunities, and therefore I am not prepared to have my opportunities increased. . . .

"How prompt we are to satisfy the hunger & thirst of our bodies; how slow to satisfy the hunger & thirst of our *souls*. Indeed we who would be practical folks cannot use this word without blushing because of our infidelity, having starved this substance almost to a shadow. We feel it to be as absurd as if a man were to break forth into a eulogy on *his dog* who hasn't any. An ordinary man will work every day for a year at shovelling dirt to support his body, or a family of bodies, but he is an extraordinary man who will work a whole day in a year for the support of his soul."

Thoreau's home life at this time, as well as his life in the woods, was happily harmonious. He often took members of the family on boat rides and chronicled the little adventures of these rides faithfully, as on the occasion in May, 1853, when he and Sophia rowed past "Mr. Prichard's land, where the river is bordered by a row of elms and low willows, at 6 P.M." and "heard a singular note of distress as it were from a catbird"—which resulted in their rescue of a kitten and its addition to the household. Moreover, he took a more active part in the pencil-making

115

business by turning his hand to an improvement in the graphite—or plumbago—used by the Thoreaus in their business.

On September 13 of that year Thoreau made a second trip to the Maine woods. This time his guide was an Indian, Joe Aitteon—"a good-looking Indian, twenty-four years old, apparently of unmixed blood, short and stout, with a broad face and reddish complexion, and eyes, methinks, narrower and more turned up at the outer corners than ours . . ." He could thus pursue his "special interest" in Indian lore at the same time that he gathered further data on the wilderness about which he planned more essays and lectures.

The goal this time was Chesuncook, just beyond the limits of Thoreau's first excursion into the Maine woods. Before reaching that lake, Thoreau lent a hand to Joe's hunting a moose, in which Thoreau's chief pleasure was the information he gained about the animal. "The distance from the tips of the hoofs of the fore-feet, stretched out, to the top of the back between the shoulders, was seven feet and five inches. . . . The extreme length was eight feet and two inches." But data about moose and hedgehogs soon gave way to rhapsodic appreciations of pine trees and night in the forest, and to Indian lore. "I asked our hosts what *Musketaquid*, the Indian name of Concord . . . meant; but they changed it to *Musketicook*, and repeated that, and Tahmunt said that it meant Dead Stream, which is probably true. *Cook* appears to mean stream, and perhaps *quid* signifies the place or ground."

The second Maine excursion lasted two weeks. By September 28, Thoreau was back in Concord, his journal filled with notes, measurements, drawings—of Indian canoes—, and the material for another lecture. In Concord

116

the elm leaves were falling, and the fringed gentian was in blossom. And in Concord he had at last to face a melancholy problem which had been pressed upon him from time to time by the publisher ("falsely so-called"), who had brought out *A Week on the Concord and Merrimack Rivers* in 1849.

The indisputable fact was that Thoreau's book had not sold at all well. It had come out like a woodland flower and remained unplucked, with but the modest appreciation of a few passersby. Since Thoreau had himself paid for the publication of the book, unsold copies belonged to him. The publisher, Munroe, had written Thoreau from time to time asking what disposition he should make of the unsold copies. At length he wrote that October that he could use the room they occupied in storage. Thoreau wrote at last and instructed him to send them— 250 bound copies, and 450 sets of sheets—to Concord.

On October 28 Thoreau wrote philosophically that "they have arrived to-day by express, filling the man's wagon,—706 copies out of an edition of 1000 which I bought of Munroe four years ago and have been ever since paying for, and have not quite paid for yet. The wares are sent to me at last, and I have an opportunity to examine my purchase. They are something more substantial than fame, as my back knows, which has borne them up two flights of stairs to a place similar to that to which they trace their origin. Of the remaining two hundred and ninety and odd, seventy-five were given away, the rest sold. I have now a library of nearly nine hundred volumes, over seven hundred of which I wrote myself. Is it not well that the author should behold the fruits of his labor? My works are piled up on one side of my chamber half as high as my head, my *opera omnia*. This is authorship; these are the work of my brain. There was just one piece of good luck in the venture. The unbound were tied up by the printer four years ago in stout paper wrappers, and inscribed,—

H. D. Thoreau's
Concord River
50 cops.

So Munroe had only to cross out 'River' and write 'Mass.' and deliver them to the expressman at once. I can see now what I write for, the result of my labors.

"Nevertheless, in spite of this result, sitting beside the inert mass of my works, I take up my pen to-night to record what thought or experience I may have had, with as much satisfaction as ever. Indeed, I believe that this result is more inspiring and better for me than if a thousand had bought my wares. It affects my privacy less and leaves me freer."

He was not quite free of this initial venture in publishing. He was still in debt $100, and this had to be paid off. Before he had settled this debt, he "was obliged to manufacture a thousand dollars' worth of pencils and slowly dispose of and finally sacrifice them." Even a man with considerably more self-confidence than Thoreau might have grown discouraged.

CHAPTER 8

Walden

If one listens to the faintest but constant suggestions of his genius, which are certainly true, he sees not to what extremes, or even insanity, it may lead him; and yet that way, as he grows more resolute and faithful, his road lies. The faintest assured objection which one healthy man feels will at length prevail over the arguments and customs of mankind. No man ever followed his genius till it misled him. Though the result were bodily weakness, yet perhaps no one can say that the consequences were to be regretted, for these were a life in conformity to higher principles. If the day and the night are such that you greet them with joy, and life emits a fragrance like flowers and sweet-scented herbs, is more elastic, more starry, more immortal,—that is your success. All nature is your congratulation, and you have cause momentarily to bless yourself. The greatest gains and values are farthest from being appreciated. We easily come to doubt if they exist. We soon forget them. They are the highest reality. Perhaps the facts most astounding and most real are never communicated by man to man. The true harvest of my daily life is somewhat as intangible and indescribable as the tints of morning or evening. It is a little star-dust caught, a segment of the rainbow which I have clutched. —WALDEN

FAR from being discouraged by the failure of his first book, Thoreau anticipated the publication of his second. Thoreau had been in correspondence with Ticknor & Fields of Boston about *Walden, or Life in the Woods* during late 1853; by early 1854, Thoreau had been advised that Ticknor & Fields planned to publish the book later that year, so that, when Horace Greeley wrote him early in March to ask that he collect and arrange his miscellaneous lectures and articles in the hope of finding a publisher to bring them out in book form, Thoreau was delighted to be able to tell Greeley that *Walden* was soon to appear. Thoreau pointed out that the publishers had not yet announced the book, but its acceptance was certain.

Greeley replied, "I shall announce it at once, whether Ticknor does or not." Further, Greeley made plans to publish excerpts from the book with the intention of arousing public interest in a book which Ticknor described to his firm's agent in London as "no common book. . . . It belongs to the same class of works with Mr. Emerson's writings & will be likely to attract attention."

Perhaps Thoreau felt that publication of a second book might gain him, if not prestige, some further respect—not that it could have mattered very much to him. For all that he had once taught and did some writing and lectured, Thoreau was hardly more to Concord than an assistant at pencil-making and a surveyor. These were the occupations which were visible and which earned him fees admissible as earnings to his townsmen.

Thoreau could have had no illusions about his status. A post-office loafer once taunted him, together with Emerson and Channing, as "the walkers." Thoreau asked, "Do you miss any of your wood?" and was told, "No, I hain't worried any yet." And Sam Staples ("whom I

120

never call Sam, however") thought nothing of calling out to Thoreau casually, "Thoreau, are you going up the street pretty soon? Well, just take a couple of these hand-bills along and drop one in at Hoar's piazza and one at Holbrook's, and I'll do as much for you another time." Thoreau could write in his journal, "There is some advantage in being the humblest, cheapest, least dignified man in the village, so that the very stable boys shall damn you. Methinks I enjoy that advantage to an unusual extent. There is many a coarsely well-meaning fellow, who knows only the skin of me, who addresses me familiarly by my Christian name. I get the whole good of him and lose nothing myself."

Apart from such a wry note or two in the course of his journal, Thoreau left no evidence to suggest that he was unduly troubled by the impression he might make on his townsmen or the wider world, and he was very probably surprised when Charles Scribner wrote to him that May asking for biographical and bibliographical data to be published in a new Scribner book, *An Encyclopaedia of American Literature*. He went on about his business—surveying, doing some good turns for the Irish who seemed to be in constant if cheerful need, inspecting fences and streams, keeping account of thunderstorms and the arrival and departure of birds, collecting a cicada he could not certainly identify and sending it to Thaddeus Harris at Cambridge to be identified, only to be asked for further specimens.

And, as always, he walked—usually in the afternoon, but now increasingly at twilight and by moonlight. They were not always bucolic idyls. Thoreau once called them "those rough all-day walks across lots?— . . . picking our way over quaking meadows and swamps and occasionally slipping into the muddy batter midleg deep; jumping or fording ditches and brooks; forcing our way through dense blueberry swamps, where there is water beneath and bushes above; then brushing through extensive birch forests all covered with green lice, which cover our clothes and face; then, relieved, under larger wood, more open beneath, steering for some more conspicuous trunk; now along a rocky hillside where the sweet-fern grows for a mile, then over a recent cutting, finding our uncertain footing on the cracking tops and trimmings of trees left by the choppers; now taking a step or two of smooth walking across a highway; now through a dense pine wood, descending into a rank, dry swamp, where the cinnamon fern rises above your head, with isles of poison-dogwood; now up a scraggy hill covered with shrub oak, stooping and winding one's way for half a mile, tearing one's clothes in many places and putting out one's eyes, and finding at last that it has no bare brow, but another slope of the same character; now through a corn-field diagonally with the rows; now coming upon the hidden melon-patch; seeing the back side of familiar hills and not knowing them. . . ."

On the ninth of August *Walden* was published. It was produced by Ticknor & Fields at a cost of 43 cents a copy, to sell for a dollar. Almost at once it brought a disciple to Thoreau—one Daniel Ricketson of New Bedford. He wrote to Thoreau three days after publication of *Walden,* writing him the kind of letter every author is gratified to receive. He hastened "to thank you for the great degree of satisfaction" *Walden* had given him. "I hail with pleasure every original production in literature which bears the stamp of a genuine and earnest love for the true philosophy of human life.—Such I assure you I esteem your book to be. To many, and to most, it will appear to be the wild musings of an eccentric and strange mind . . .

122

But to me the book appears to evince a mind most thoroughly self possessed, highly cultivated with a strong vein of common sense. The whole book is a prose poem . . . and at the same time as simple as a running brook." He addressed Thoreau as "Dear Mr. Walden," and echoed Thoreau in his long letter—"O how much we lose by civilization!"

Even before the book's publication, Horace Greeley had published a summary and more than three columns of extracts from *Walden*. This generous space devoted to the book in so widely-read a newspaper undoubtedly sent the book off to a modest start in sales; it gave much more of a sampling of Thoreau than any review could have done. Other reviews were less generous, but on the whole, favorable. *Graham's Magazine* called Thoreau a Transcendentalist, one of those people "who lay the greatest stress on the 'I'." *Putnam's* wondered why, if Thoreau liked the Walden experiment so much, he did not "stick to it?" and carped a little about his book, but on the whole pronounced it a good book—"there have been a good many lives spent and a good deal of noise made about them, too, from the sum total of whose results not half so much good could be extracted as may be found in this little volume. Many a man will find pleasure in it, and many a one, we hope, will be profited by its counsels. A tour in Europe would have cost a good deal more, and not have produced half as much. . . . We heartily recommend . . . him to the class of readers who extract thoughts as well as words from an author . . ." And Edwin Morton of the class of 1855, reviewing both Thoreau's books in the *Harvard Magazine*, thought *Walden* "less artistic than its predecessor," but called both of them "rare books," while an anonymous reviewer in *The Knickerbocker*, sneering at town and rural humbugs, nevertheless conceded that *Walden* "should be extensively read" because "it encourages the belief, which in this utilitarian age enough needs encouragement, that there is some other object to live for except 'to make money.' "

Walden was Thoreau's *apologia* for his way of life. It was meant to contain more of his philosophy, as plainly set forth as he could set it forth, than his first book. It was not intended for people who were satisfied with their lives as much as for those who lived "lives of quiet desperation." Out of his journal and the Walden experience Thoreau put into his book his thoughts on four central themes—the economic condition of men, life close to nature and its rewards, the "higher laws" man understands through a life close to nature, and the quiet desperation of the lives so many men lead. It was never meant for idle readers who did not want to be made to think, and it could be little appreciated by anyone who did not also, like Thoreau, value nonconformity and individuality.

Yet for Thoreau, by all the evidence, the book was an accomplished thing, and thus in a sense a closed chapter in his life. His lengthy journal for that summer is concerned with many things—the flight of an eagle, the nest of a snapping turtle, a nighthawk, harvest flies, river clams, the great fringed orchis, the sheen of the fields, the opening of flowers, the necessity of privacy ("My attic chamber has compelled me to sit below with the family at evening for a month. I feel the necessity of deepening the stream of my life; I must cultivate privacy. It is very dissipating to be with people too much. . . . I cannot spare my moonlight and my mountains for the best of man I am likely to get in exchange."), sailing on Fair Haven, the sting of a wasp, and scores of other subjects,

124

most notably the affair of the slave, Anthony Burns—but of *Walden* there was set down only the briefest of notes, under date of August 9, " 'Walden' published," though perhaps his entry of September 2 was intended to be related to the book—"My faults are: / Paradoxes,—saying just the opposite,—a style which may be imitated. / Ingenius. / Playing with words,—getting the laugh,—not always simple, strong, and broad. / Using current phrases and maxims, when I should speak for myself. / Not always earnest. / 'in short,' 'in fact,' 'alas!' etc. / Want of conciseness."—however applicable these words might have been to his lectures—and neither of these entries was included in proper sequence in the body of the journal; both were written on the inside cover page of the manuscript, and may not have been intended as integral portions of the journal.

The affair of Anthony Burns was similar to that of Sims. Burns, another runaway Negro slave, had been arrested in Boston and returned to Virginia in a government cutter, in May of that year. Thoreau's reaction spilled over in the pages of the journal, and at length; it did more—out of his cold fury, Thoreau assembled from his notes on both the Sims and Burns cases, a fiery paper which he delivered under the title of *Slavery in Massachusetts* as an address before the Anti-Slavery Convention meeting in Framingham, Massachusetts, on Independence Day, and which William Lloyd Garrison then published on July 21 in the *Liberator*.

It was an address that brought Thoreau more reaction than *Walden* did, for the time being. Thoreau's attack was against the moral weakness of the North, not against slavery, for of slavery as an institution he did not profess to know enough to speak. "The whole military force of the State is at the service of a Mr. Suttle, a slaveholder from Virginia, to enable him to catch a man whom he calls his property; but not a soldier is offered to save a citizen of Massachusetts from being kidnapped!" he cried. "The law will never make men free; it is men who have got to make the law free. . . . I would remind my countrymen that they are to be men first, and Americans only at a late and convenient hour. . . . I feel that, to some extent, the State has fatally interfered with my lawful business. . . . We have used up all our inherited freedom. If we would save our lives, we must fight for them." Thoreau was still hearing about his Framingham lecture two months after publication of *Walden*.

In the meantime, Thoreau had met another young writer who was to become a lifelong correspondent. This was Thomas Cholmondeley of England. He had come to Concord primarily to visit Emerson that summer but found himself much taken by Thoreau, and began to take walks with Thoreau. He was still in the vicinity—"staying at our house," Thoreau wrote to Blake—in October, asking Thoreau "to teach him *botany*—i.e., anything which I know—and also to make an excursion to some mountains with him." He proposed to Blake that Cholmondeley might come along to visit Blake when Thoreau went, bound to walk to Wachusett, a proposal Blake eagerly accepted.

On October 19th Thoreau left for Westminster by train, and with Blake walked the six miles to the top of Wachusett where, the following morning, they "Saw the sun rise from the mountain-top. . . . It was worth the while to see westward the countless hills and fields all apparently flat, now white with frost. A little white fog marked the site of many a lake and the course of the Nashua, and in the east horizon the great pond had its own fog mark in a long, low bank of cloud." It must have been a nostalgic walk, reminding Thoreau of his first walk there in May, 1842, when he had set down a poem to celebrate Wachusett, "who like me / Standest alone without society."

Daniel Ricketson constantly urged Thoreau to visit him at New Bedford, where Ricketson spent a great deal of his time in a shanty—"in study and meditation," as Ricketson told Thoreau. Ricketson bore a certain kinship to Thoreau, but he was more gregarious, more inclined to seek out people, whereas Thoreau gave the impression of only tolerating the company of others. Later that year Thoreau visited New Bedford and Ricketson, who lived near the Acushnet River north of the town, and, as usual, took notes on the setting, which, though in latitude only different "about a degree" was "far more in climate."

But, such occasional visits away from Concord notwithstanding, it was Concord and its environs which Thoreau traveled with the greatest pleasure and the continuing affection he had had for this place all his life. He surveyed between visits, he sailed to Ball's Hill with Channing, paddled up river to Clamshell, walked to Walden along the railroad or by way of Hubbard Bridge, went up the north bank of the Assabet with Channing, skated up river to Fair Haven—again with Channing whose "skates are not the best," and who was "beside . . ." a "far from an easy skater, so that, as he said, it was killing work for him. Time and again the perspiration actually dropped from his forehead on to the ice, and it froze in long icicles on his beard. Yet he kept up his spirits and his fun, said he had seen much more suffering than I . . ."

Thoreau's sympathy was limited. He was a sprightly skater himself, capable of leaping aloft and cavorting on the ice, and his interests were in the face of the country. "The shadows on the snow are indigo-blue. The pines look very dark. The white oak leaves are a cinnamon-color, the black and red (?) oak leaves a reddish brown or leather-color. I see mice and rabbit and fox tracks on the meadow. Once a partridge rises from the alders and skims across the river at its widest part . . . I see the track of an otter made since yesterday morning. How glorious the perfect stillness and peace of the winter landscape!"

Meanwhile, *Walden* was selling slowly but steadily, and an awareness of Thoreau as a writer was growing. Charles Sumner, later Senator from Massachusetts, wrote from Boston that reading only the early chapters of the book satisfied him that Thoreau had "made a contribution to the permanent literature of our mother tongue," and from Fr. Adrien Rouquette the author of *Walden* received a gift of three volumes of Rouquette's work, including Rouquette's *Wild Flowers;* in return, Thoreau sent him a complimentary copy of *A Week on the Concord and Merrimack Rivers,* a book for which an increasing number of readers of *Walden* were beginning to ask.

When Cholmondeley left Concord in November, he carried with him letters of introduction from Thoreau to Bronson Alcott and Dr. Thaddeus W. Harris, the Harvard librarian, for whom Thoreau had been gathering grubs, and from whom he had been borrowing such books as Wilson's translation of the *Vishnoo Purana.* Cholmondeley was bound for home and involvement in the Crimean War, and Thoreau that late autumn and winter went on a series of lectures.

He lectured first in Philadelphia, and hoped thereafter for an invitation to make a Western tour. It was not forthcoming. The Library Association of Akron, Ohio, asked him to lecture there, but since there were no other inquiries from the middle west, Thoreau would not go. Instead, he prepared a new lecture. He went through his voluminous journal for 1854 and wrote *Getting a Living,* which was later to become more widely known as *Life without Principle.*

This lecture was for Thoreau what *Self-Reliance* was for Emerson. It was a statement of Thoreau's philosophy. It was a Transcendental attack on materialism, in the course of which Thoreau also struck at public opinion and the influence of organized religion. It was a strong plea for fundamental principles—that is, the principles Thoreau recognized as valid. It was a good, sound lecture, though Thoreau's contempt for the way of life chosen by the mass of men in their desire for wealth or fame or whatever worthless will-o-the-wisp they followed all their years, shone through.

He expressed his bitterness at being told what to lecture about, as he sometimes was. "I take it for granted, when I am invited to lecture anywhere . . . that there is a desire to hear what *I think* on some subject, though I may be the greatest fool in the country, and not that I should say pleasant things merely, or such as the audience will assent to; and I resolve, accordingly, that I will give them a strong dose of myself."

He decried "the way in which we spend our lives. . . . I think that there is nothing, not even crime, more opposed to poetry, to philosophy, ay, to life itself, than this incessant business. . . . If a man walk in the woods for love of them half of each day, he is in danger of being regarded as a loafer; but if he spends his whole day as a speculator, shearing off those woods and making earth bald before her time, he is esteemed an industrious and

129

enterprising citizen. As if a town had no interest in its forests but to cut them down!"

His contempt for money as an end in itself was made bitterly clear. "I have been surprised when one has with confidence proposed to me, a grown man, to embark in some enterprise of his, as if I had absolutely nothing to do, my life having been a complete failure hitherto." And he publicly prized his freedom. "Perhaps I am more than usually jealous with respect to my freedom. I feel that my connection with and obligation to society are still very slight and transient. Those slight labors which afford me a livelihood, and by which it is allowed that I am to some extent serviceable to my contemporaries, are as yet commonly a pleasure to me, and I am not often reminded that they are a necessity. So far I am successful. But I foresee that if my wants should be much increased, the labor required to supply them would become a drudgery. If I should sell both my forenoons and afternoons to society, as most appear to do, I am sure that for me there would be nothing left worth living for. I trust that I shall never thus sell my birthright for a mess of pottage."

He held that the gold-rush to California reflected "the greatest disgrace on mankind. That so many are ready to live by luck, and so get the means of commanding the labor of others less lucky, without contributing any value to society! And that is called enterprise!" and added that, after reading Howitt's account of Australian gold mining, "I was thinking, accidentally, of my own unsatisfactory life, doing as others do; and with that vision of the diggings still before me, I asked myself why *I* might not be washing some gold daily, though it were only the finest particles—why *I* might not sink a shaft down to the gold within me, and work that mine. *There* is a Ballarat, a Bendigo for you—what though it were a sulky-gully? At any rate, I might pursue some path, however solitary and narrow and crooked, in which I could walk with love and reverence. Wherever a man separates from the multitude, and goes his own way in this mood, there indeed is a fork in the road, though ordinary travelers may see only a gap in the paling. His solitary path across lots will turn out the *higher way* of the two. . . . A man had better starve at once than lose his innocence in the process of getting his bread."

He scorned the press, he ridiculed the concept of freedom that prevailed in the nation. "Do we call this the land of the free? What is it to be free from King George and continue the slaves of King Prejudice? What is it to be born free and not to live free? What is the value of any political freedom, but as a means to moral freedom? Is it a freedom to be slaves, or a freedom to be free, of which we boast? We are a nation of politicians, concerned about the outmost defenses only of freedom. It is our children's children who may perchance be really free. We tax ourselves unjustly. There is a part of us which is not represented. It is taxation without representation. We quarter troops, we quarter fools and cattle of all sorts upon ourselves. We quarter our gross bodies on our poor souls, till the former eat up all the latter's substance."

While this lecture was not stylistically the equal of *Walden,* yet it remained the most succinct statement of Thoreau's principles. He wrote a footnote to it to Blake in mid-December: "The world rests on principles. The wise gods will never make underpinning of a man. But as long as he crouches, and skulks, and shirks his work, every creature that has weight will be treading on his toes and crushing him; he will himself tread with one foot on the other foot."

Thoreau first delivered this lecture at New Bedford the day after Christmas, 1854. In order to make the personal acquaintance of Daniel Ricketson, he went to New Bedford the day before. Ricketson was clearing snow before his house when Thoreau came, clad in a long, dark overcoat, wearing a soft dark hat, and carrying in one hand an umbrella, in the other a portmanteau. "As he came near to me I gave him the usual salutation," wrote Ricketson in his memoirs. He supposed Thoreau to be "either a pedlar or some way-traveller." Subsequently, he sketched Thoreau in his traveling clothes, one of the few such sketches of Thoreau extant.

The two men were congenial. Thoreau at New Bedford—and on the 28th of December at Nantucket, where he delivered his new lecture for the second time—filled his journal with notes about the region. He did not neglect a partial listing of Ricketson's library, stressing the many wood-engravings by Bewick illustrating books on Ricketson's shelves. The weather in New Bedford delighted him. ("It was wonderfully warm and pleasant . . . I felt the winter breaking up in me . . .") He traveled to Nantucket in misty rain, which continued throughout the day of his lecture there, though he went about in it and examined some of Captain Gardiner's experiments in raising pine trees.

Of what his audiences thought of his lecture there is no record. One can imagine their reaction. Hold up a man's morals for scrutiny and he will laugh with you; but ridicule his love of money or fame and you cut into a sensitive nerve indeed.

On the 29th Thoreau left Nantucket early in the morning for Concord in a fog "so thick that we were lost on the water. . . . Whistled and listened for the locomotive's answer, but probably heard only the echo of our own whistle at first, but at last the locomotive's whistle and the life-boat bell."

By the end of the month he was again on the river to Fair Haven Pond, celebrating the glory of the winter landscape.

CHAPTER 9

Surveyor of Concord

Live in each season as it passes; breathe the air, drink the drink, taste the fruit, and resign yourself to the influences of each. Let them be your only diet drink and botanical medicines. In August live on berries, not dried meats and pemmican, as if you were in shipboard making your way through a waste ocean, or in a northern desert. Be blown on by all the winds. Open all your pores and bathe in all the tides of Nature, in all her streams and oceans, at all seasons. Miasma and infection are from within, not without. The invalid, brought to the brink of the grave by an unnatural life, instead of imbibing only the great influence that Nature is, drinks only the tea made of a particular herb, while he still continues his unnatural life,—saves at the spile and wastes at the bung. He does not love Nature or his life, and so sickens and dies, and no doctor can cure him. Grow green with spring, yellow and ripe with autumn. Drink of each season's influence as a vial, a true panacea of all remedies mixed for your especial use. The vials of summer never made a man sick, but those which he stored in his cellar. Drink the wines, not of your bottling, but Nature's bottling; not kept in goat-skins or pig-skins, but the skins of a myriad fair berries. Let Nature do your bottling and your pickling and preserving. For all Nature is doing her best each moment to make us well. She exists for no other end. Do not resist her. With the least inclination to be well, we should not be sick.

134

Men have discovered—or think they have dis-
covered—the salutariness of a few wild things only,
and not of all nature. Why, 'nature' is but another
name for health, and the seasons are but different
states of health. Some men think that they are
not well in spring, or summer, or autumn, or win-
ter; it is only because they are not well in them.

—JOURNAL, 1853

HALF way through this thirty-eighth year of his life, Thoreau was at his peak of energy and good spirits; before he had completed it, his strength had begun to ebb, and he was not thereafter to regain the fine health he had known most of his adult life. He began the year with a lecture at Worcester—presumably *Getting a Living*—and noted that the Antiquarian Library in that city "is richer in pamphlets and newspapers than Harvard."

The first report he had on the subject matter of this lecture came to hand a few days after his return from Worcester. Ricketson wrote him: "I have heard several sensible people speak well of your lecture before the New Bedford Lyceum, but conclude it was not generally understood." This was perhaps not more than Thoreau had expected.

During that first month of 1855 Thoreau saw the pleasant review of his work published in the *Harvard Magazine*. Subsequently, while in Cambridge, Thoreau stopped at Holworthy Hall to call on the editor, F. B. Sanborn. In Sanborn's absence, he left a copy of *A Week on the Concord and Merrimack Rivers* for the writer of the review. Sanborn was at that time a senior in college. Though he saw Thoreau not long after Thoreau's call at Holworthy Hall, when Thoreau came into the library where Sanborn then was, he had not known that Tho-

135

reau had called on him. He wrote to Thoreau on the thirtieth, asking to "seek" him out when next he came to Concord.

Of *Walden* he wrote to thank Thoreau "for the new light it shows me the aspects of Nature in, and for the marvelous beauty of your descriptions," though he did not think Thoreau's philosophy "worth a straw." Thoreau replied to Sanborn that he would be glad to welcome him at any time in Concord. Within two months Sanborn was not only visiting Thoreau; he was seeing him frequently, for he had taken over the teaching of school in Concord, and was soon taking his meals at the Thoreau house. Teaching, however, was not Sanborn's only occupation; with almost clinical interest he was compiling notes on the lives and activities of those people who made Concord what he had called, when writing from Cambridge, "a sort of Mecca for our pilgrimages," —Emerson, Channing, and Thoreau chief among them.

Economically, Thoreau's position had now improved to the extent that he need not any longer worry about how to make ends meet and still do very much as he liked. Though the sales of pencils had fallen off, the demand for graphite had increased to such a point that the Thoreau family had moved up a notch or two in the social scale of Concord. Contributing even more to Thoreau's satisfaction was the steady sale of *Walden*, which, within a year of publication had sold over a thousand copies and had stimulated enough of a demand for *A Week on the Concord and Merrimack Rivers* to impel Thoreau to propose to Ticknor & Fields that it might be time to republish that book, though there were still copies of the first and only edition to be had from Thoreau and from his current publishers, who had been getting ten copies at a time from Thoreau's stock in the attic room.

Thoreau could now, in view of his improved circumstances, enjoy the Concord countryside to the full. Small wonder that on a day of winter thaw he could write ecstatically in his journal, "Perhaps what most moves us in winter is some reminiscence of far-off summer. How we leap by the side of the open brooks! What beauty in the running brooks! What life! What society! The cold is merely superficial; it is summer still at the core, far, far within. It is in the cawing of the crow, the crowing of the cock, the warmth of the sun on our backs. . . . It mingles with the slight murmur of the village, the sound of children at play, as one stream empties gently into another, and the wild and tame are one. . . . Ah, bless the Lord, O my soul! bless him for wildness, for crows that will not alight within gunshot! and bless him for hens, too, that croak and cackle in the yards!"

He went out into the country around Concord almost daily, save only on those days when he went to Cambridge or perhaps to Boston, after books, or to carry specimens to Harris. He skated often for many miles, especially delighting to do so in gently falling snow, and did not mind on occasion skating "into a crack" and sliding "on my side twenty-five feet." He enjoyed walking in snowstorms, with Channing or by himself, especially in deep woods where the snow "had lodged not only on the oak leaves and the evergreens, but on every twig and branch . . . the trunks also being plastered with snow, a peculiar soft light was diffused around, very unlike the ordinary darkness of the forest, as if you were inside a drift or snow house."

He made diagrams of snow drifts to illustrate his notes

and measured the rise and fall of the river and the brooks, especially during freshets. "It is surprising how much work will be accomplished in . . . a night, . . . so many a brook will have run itself out and now be found reduced within reasonable bounds." He made drawings of birds, of pine cones and scales, of animal tracks, of ice cakes and worm borings and grains of ice. He caught a flying squirrel with the intention of taming it; he failed, and released it again. He made careful studies of the notes of birds, and one March day he tried to imitate the honking of geese in an effort to attract them: "I found myself flapping my sides with my elbows, as with wings, and uttering something like the syllables *mow-ack* with a nasal twang and twist in my head; and I produced their note so perfectly in the opinion of hearers that I thought I might possibly draw a flock down."—an opinion which the geese moving north evidently did not share.

He kept all his usual records—of the first frogs, the first redwing, the first bluebird to be seen or heard—all first things, indeed ("The skunk-cabbage open yesterday,—the earliest flower this season. . . . Some twenty minutes after sundown I hear the first *booming* of a snipe. . . . At sunset after the rain, the robins and song sparrows fill the air along the river with their song."). On one day he found a dead merganser, not long since shot; he took it home ("a perfectly fresh and very beautiful bird, and as I raise it, I get sight of its long, slender vermilion bill (color of red sealing-wax) and its clean, bright-orange legs and feet, and then of its perfectly smooth and spotlessly pure white breast and belly, tinged with a faint salmon . . ."), and stuffed it ("It is wonderful that a man, having undertaken such an enterprise,

138

ever persevered in it to the end, and equally wonderful that he succeeded.'').

He was continuing to be, and proud to be, as he put it in *Walden,* "anxious to improve the nick of time, and notch it" on his stick, "to stand on the meeting of two eternities, the past and future, which is precisely the present moment." He was still, as always, "reporter to a journal, of no very wide circulation . . . self-appointed inspector of snow-storms and rain-storms . . . surveyor . . . of forest paths and all across-lots routes, keeping them open, and ravines bridged and passable at all seasons, where the public heel had testified to their utility. . . ." with "an eye to the unfrequented nooks and corners of the farm." He was faithfully minding his "business, till it became more and more evident that my townsmen would not after all admit me into the list of town officers, nor make my place a sinecure with a modest allowance."

Nevertheless, eccentric though they may have thought Thoreau, accustomed as they were to thinking him a loafer and a college graduate who had thrown away his "chances," Thoreau's townsmen accepted him for what he was.

But the spring of 1855 was not all balm and delight. Perhaps, as Miss Minott said Dr. Spring had told her, "when the sap began to come up into the trees . . . then the diseases of the human body come out. The idea is that man's body sympathizes with the rest of nature, and his pent-up humors burst forth like the sap from wounded trees. This with the mass may be that languor or other weakness commonly called spring feelings." What troubled Thoreau that April and thereafter for some months was not spring fever, however, nor was it

139

only bronchitis. It was a general weakness, amounting to a decline in his health, which affected his legs and made walking—his greatest pleasure—doubly difficult. Yet he persisted in it and would not be daunted, though he betrayed a certain melancholy from time to time in his notes, and told Blake he had been "good for nothing but to lie on my back and wait for something to turn up."

He added, "I should feel a little less ashamed if I could give any name to my disorder, but I cannot, and our doctor cannot help me to it, and I will not take the name of any disease in vain. However, there is one consolation in being sick, and that is the possibility that you may recover to a better state than you were ever in before. I expected in the winter to be deep in the woods of Maine in my canoe long before this, but I am so far from that that I can only take a languid walk in Concord streets." This in June. Maine was out of the question, but within a month he did go with Channing to Cape Cod to sit in the sun and hope that this might improve his health and vaporize his melancholy.

The illness might possibly have been an assault upon his lungs. It could have been brought about by the inhalation of the graphite dust which was the core of the Thoreau business which now supported Cynthia and John, Sophia and Henry comfortably. It was not until the year was almost out that Thoreau regained the assurance he hoped for in his legs. Yet he was not the same in strength; he was never to be in the same health as he had been before the onset of the illness, though he was not to be put off from his continuing exploration of Concord and its environs.

That spring, too, Thoreau was involved in another struggle with an editor. George William Curtis had accepted for publication Thoreau's account of Cape Cod, which Curtis proposed to run in five chapters in *Putnam's*. Curtis thought some of Thoreau's views "heretical." Thoreau attempted at first to compromise by revising his copy. But Thoreau's revision was of style in the interests of clarity; he wanted to make his position perfectly clear, or more clear than it already was; and it was already too clear for Curtis. He could not revise his attitude or compromise with his convictions, and Curtis was too conservative to permit Thoreau their free expression for the fear—to which all editors are prone—of giving offense to many of the more conservative readers of *Putnam's*.

What Thoreau would not do, Curtis did. He made deletions in Thoreau's manuscript before sending it to the printer. This Thoreau would not tolerate. Much as he appreciated the monthly $35 stipend he received, he withdrew the balance of *Cape Cod* after three instalments had appeared in the magazine. He intended to remain a man of principle and if no further word of his appeared in print.

Meanwhile, Horace Greeley, still interested in Thoreau's place in the world of letters, wrote to urge him to send review copies of *Walden*—accompanied by copies of his first book—to the *Westminster Review* and to Dickens's *Household Words* in England, since these journals ought to print reviews of the books and perhaps find some interest among British publishers who might bring out a British edition of one or both books. George Eliot reviewed *Walden* in the *Westminster Review* within a few months, but this favorable review brought no immediate inquiry from any British publisher.

By early autumn Thoreau was beginning to regain his vigor. He was still dubious about making excursions far from Concord. He wrote Ricketson in late September, "I am so wedded to my way of spending a day—require such broad margins of leisure, and such a complete wardrobe of old clothes, that I am ill fitted for going abroad. Pleasant is it sometimes to sit, at home, on a single egg all day, in your own nest, though it may prove at last to be an egg of chalk. The old coat that I wear is Concord—it is my morning robe & study gown, my working dress and suit of ceremony, and my night-gown after all. Cleave to the simplest ever—Home—home— home. *Cars* sound like *cares* to me."

Ricketson visited him, and later, Blake, to whom he wrote after his return home: "Thank you! thank you for going a-wooding with me,—and enjoying it,—for being warmed by my wood fire. I have indeed enjoyed it much alone. I see how I might enjoy it yet more with company,—how we might help each other to live. And to be admitted to Nature's hearth costs nothing. None is excluded, but excludes himself. You have only to push aside the curtain. . . .

"Talk of burning your smoke after the wood has been consumed! There is a far more important and warming heat, commonly lost, which precedes the burning of the wood. It is the smoke of industry, which is incense. I had been so thoroughly warmed in body and spirit, that when at length my fuel was housed, I came near selling it to the ash-man, as if I had extracted all its heat."

By late November Thoreau had recovered his health sufficiently to go boating and to load a pine log from the Assabet into his boat so that he could take it home and make wheels "to roll my boat into winter quarters upon. So I sawed off two thick rollers from one end, pierced them for wheels, and then of a joist which I had found drifting on the river in the summer I made an axletree,

142

and on this I rolled my boat out." Boating afforded him much pleasure, and made up in part for the absence of the long walks he had abandoned for the duration of his illness. Very often, those visitors he could not persuade to go sauntering with him, could readily enough be induced to go boating. Writing later, George Curtis recalled boating with Thoreau as one of the "most vivid recollections of my life in Concord." They had gone boating one evening and went along the river in the darkness. "We lighted a huge fire of fat pine in an iron crate beyond the bow of the boat and drifted slowly through an illuminated circle of the ever-changing aspect of the river bed."

On Indian Summer days that November he could not keep to the house. "It is akin to sin to spend such a day in the house," he wrote in his journal. "This, too, is the *recovery* of the year,—as if the year, having nearly or quite accomplished its work, and abandoned all design, were in a more favorable and poetic mood, and thought rushed in to fill the vacuum. . . ." He was much on the river, watching for tortoises, blue herons, bitterns, and enjoying the water. "This is the aspect under which the Musketaquid might be represented at this season: a long, smooth lake, reflecting the bare willows and button-bushes, the stubble, and the wool-grass on its tussock, a muskrat-cabin or two conspicuous on its margin amid the unsightly tops of pontederia, and a bittern disappearing on undulating wing around a bend."

On the last day of that month, Thoreau received through Nichols & Company of Boston a shipment of books Thomas Cholmondeley had selected for him. They had been dispatched by Chapman of London, since Cholmondeley had gone to the Crimea, as he had expected to do. Knowing of Thoreau's interest in Indian literature and thought, Cholmondeley had gone to considerable pains to assemble a shelf of books for Thoreau. The shelf included Wilson's *Rig Veda Sanhita,* a translation of the *Mandukya Upanishads,* Wilson's *Vishnu Purana,* Haughton's *Institutes of Menu,* the *Sankhya Karika,* the *Bhagavat Geeta,* Wilson's *Sakuntala,* the *Bhagavita Purana,* the Chevalier Bunsen's *Christianity and Mankind,* and others.

Thoreau was delighted to have them. He built cases for them made in part of driftwood he had salvaged from the Concord River, and wrote Cholmondeley to thank him for his "princely gift." To Blake he wrote, "I have not made out the significance of this godsend yet," though he had "not dipped far into the new ones yet."

Welcome as the books were, they came at a time when Thoreau would have little opportunity to read. Having regained the confidence in his legs that he had almost lost during the travail of his inexplicable illness, he was up and about that winter as often as he might be. Even days of sub-zero weather did not keep him in the house, nor did deep snow. That winter of 1855–1856 was a winter of very heavy snow. At one time Thoreau carefully measured sixteen inches on the level, and by the time the snow was decreasing, he noted in his journal that for a two month period beginning early in January there had never been less than a foot of snow on the level in the environs of Concord.

He went out in all weather, even daring the biting northwest wind in sub-zero weather. He had now grown a beard, a sort of Quaker beard, covering his throat. He was photographed early in 1856 in Worcester, by D. B. Maxham, who took on that occasion the most often-reproduced photograph of Thoreau. Beards were at that

144

time coming back into fashion, but it is unlikely that Thoreau grew one for any other reason but to protect his throat on his frequent hiking excursions.

He needed such protection that winter, for he had not, in fact, so much regained his former health as improved upon his recent condition. He could not in truth say of his physical condition what he could write of his financial circumstances that January in his journal: "Within the last five years I have had the command of a little more money than in the previous five years, for I have sold some books and some lectures; yet I have not been a whit better fed or clothed or warmed or sheltered, not a whit richer, except that I have been less concerned about my living, but perhaps my life has been the less serious for it, and, to balance it, I feel now that there is a possibility of failure." Nothing was set down in his journal about the modest success of *Walden*, though he wrote Calvin Greene in Michigan that *Walden* had now sold over two thousand copies, in "an audience of excellent character . . . I should consider it a greater success to interest one wise and earnest soul, than a million unwise & frivolous."

His journal is filled with his accounts of Nature in Concord, and his thoughts rooted in Nature, with measurements of trees, snow depths, ice depths, records of his walking out and what he saw on such excursions—how the weeds looked against the snow, and the sunsets ("The colors of the west seem more than usually warm, perhaps by contrast with this simple snow-clad earth over which we look and the clear cold sky,—a sober but extensive redness, almost every night passing into a dun."), how the sap ran from the sugar maples and how he made maple sugar ("I put in saleratus and a little milk while boiling, the former to neutralize the acid, and the latter

145

to collect the impurities in a skum. After boiling it till I burned it a little, and my small quantity would not flow when cool, but was as hard as half-done candy, I put it on again, and in a minute it was softened and turned to sugar.").

He attended the felling of a giant old Concord elm—"so to speak, the funeral of this old citizen of the town,—I who commonly do not attend funerals,—as it became me to do. I was the chief if not the only mourner there. I have taken the measure of his grandeur; have spoken a few words of eulogy at his grave, . . . But there were only the choppers and the passers-by to hear me. Further the town was not represented; the fathers of the town, the selectmen, the clergy were not there. But I have not known a fitter occasion for a sermon of late." And that same month he set down in his journal again his admiration for Emerson's paternal aunt, Miss Mary, whom he had only the previous month described to Blake as "the youngest person in Concord, though about eighty,—and the most apprehensive of a genuine thought; earnest to know of your inner life; most stimulating society; and exceedingly witty withal. She says they called her old when she was young, and she has never grown any older."

Early in March Thoreau wrote to Ricketson: "This has indeed been a grand winter for me & for all of us. I am not considering how much I have enjoyed it. What matters it how happy or unhappy we have been, if we have minded our business and advanced our affairs. I have made it a part of my business to wade in the snow & take the measure of the ice. The ice on one of our ponds was just two feet thick on the first of March—and I have to-day been surveying a wood-lot where I sank about two feet at every step."

He added that he missed Channing, who was in New

146

Bedford: " 'But O the heavy change' now he is gone!" and went on to indite a fond description of his walking companion in a memorable portrait. "The C you have seen & described is the real Simon Pure. You have seen him. Many a good ramble may you have together. You will see in him still more *of the same kind*—to attract & to puzzle you. How to serve him most effectually has long been a problem with his friends. Perhaps it is left for you to solve it. I suspect that the most that you or any one can do for him is to appreciate his genius—to buy & read, & cause others to buy & read his poems. That is the hand which he has put forth to the world—Take hold of that. Review them if you can. Perhaps take the risk of publishing something more which he may write.

"Your knowledge of Cowper will help you to know C. He will accept sympathy & aid, but he will not bear questioning—unless the aspects of the sky are particularly auspicious. He will even be 'reserved & enigmatic,' & you must deal with him at arm's length.

"I have no secrets to tell you concerning him, and do not wish to call obvious excellences & defects by far-fetched names. I think I have already spoken to you more, and more to the purpose, on this theme, than I am likely to write now—nor need I suggest how witty & poetic he is—and what an inexhaustible fund of good-fellowship you will find in him."

Later that month Thoreau's favorite uncle, Charles Dunbar, died. He was 76. He was buried next day, and Thoreau noted in his journal, "He was born in February, 1780, the winter of the Great Snow, and he dies in the winter of another great snow,—a life bounded by great snows."

That March, too, Horace Greeley wrote to suggest that Thoreau come to live with the Greeley family, to teach his two children, at Chappaqua. Thoreau did not reject the suggestion outright, and Greeley hastened to assure him "that money shall not divide us . . . I am very sure that I shall be willing to pay such sum as you will consider satisfactory." Pending the return of Mrs. Greeley from Europe, Thoreau agreed to begin his residence at Chappaqua by July first. But he did not, after all, go.

Perhaps he did not relish the prospect of further tutoring, any more than he looked forward to much lecturing. He had written Calvin Greene in May, "lecturing has commonly proved so foreign & irksome to me, that I think I could only use it to acquire the means with which to make an independent tour another time." And he wrote to Ricketson later that year, in reply to an invitation to teach during the coming winter, "I find that I cannot entertain the idea. It would require such a revolution of all my habits, I think, as would sap the very foundation of me. I am engaged to Concord & my very private pursuits by 10,000 ties, & it would be suicide to cut them. If I were weaker, & not somewhat stronger physically, I should be more tempted. I am so busy that I cannot even think of visiting you. The days are not long enough or I am not strong enough to do the work of the day before bed-time."—which very probably accounts fully for Thoreau's ultimate decision not to go to Chappaqua to live.

There were occasions, however, on which Thoreau did not do as he wanted—however few in number. One such occurred August 8, 1856, when, coming from the house "thinking to empty my boat and go a-meditating along the river," Thoreau discovered that his father's pig had escaped. "Here was an ugly duty not to be shirked,—a wild shoat that weighed but ninety to be tracked, caught, and penned,—an afternoon's work, at least (if I were lucky enough to accomplish it so soon), prepared for me, quite different from what I had anticipated." He could not ignore that duty. "Do the duty that lies nearest to thee." He began to track the pig from the corner where he escaped, "making a step of his trough." The tracks were plain enough where the pig went through the garden and along the front yard walk. Presently he caught sight of the pig up the street; unhappily, the pig also caught sight of him and led him a merry chase, through town, across lots, to the river's edge, Thoreau after him. "Each neighbor whose garden I traverse tells me some anecdote of losing pigs, or the attempt to drive them, by which I am not encouraged."

Thoreau's account of this event is filled with humor and a sense of comedy. "Twice he ran up the narrow street, for he knew I did not wish it, but though the main street was broad and open and no traveller in sight, when I tried to drive him past this opening he invariably turned his piggish head toward me, dodged from side to side, and finally ran up the narrow street or down the main one, as if there were a high barrier erected before him. But really he is no more obstinate than I. I cannot but respect his tactics and his independence. He will be he, and I may be I."

A passing Irishman was engaged to help, and the pig was finally chased into a carriage-manufactory, and after some further difficulties was roped. Driving the pig home was not easy, but Thoreau did at least get home at dark, "wet through and supperless, covered with mud and wheel-grease, without any rare flowers."

Early in September Thoreau went to Brattleboro, Vermont, to visit Charles Frost and Mary Brown. He climbed the hills there, and walked up the bank of the Connecticut River—("The Concord is worth a hundred of it for my purposes. It looks narrow as well as shallow.")—and went botanizing. He climbed Chesterfield Mountain with Frances and Mary Brown. He recorded that the most interesting thing he saw in Brattleboro "was the skin and skull of a panther . . . which was killed, according to a written notice attached, on the 15th of June by the Saranac Club of Brattleboro, six young men, on a fishing and hunting excursion. . . . I was surprised at its great size and apparent strength. It gave one a new idea of our American forests and the vigor of nature here."

He remained there five days and then went to Walpole, New Hampshire, to visit with Bronson Alcott and his family. For part of the way he walked, ascending Fall Mountain "with a heavy valise on my back." He explored the country around Alcott's house, and spent some time listing the plants he found during his week away from Concord, for by the thirteenth he was rowing up the Assabet to gather ripe grapes.

For all the vigor with which he had tramped the New England hills, he was well aware that his former strength had not fully returned, for when he wrote to Thomas Cholmondeley in October, thanking him again for the books he had sent and hinting at the coming of the Civil War ("perhaps a more serious war still is breaking out here. I seem to hear its distant mutterings, though it may be long before the bolt will fall in our midst. There has not been anything which you could call union between the North and South in this country for many years, and there cannot be so long as slavery is in the way."), he gave Cholmondeley "but a poor account" of himself.

"I got 'run down' they say," he wrote, "more than a year ago, and have not yet got fairly up again. It has

not touched my spirits however, for they are as indifferently tough, as sluggishly resilient, as a dried fungus. I
would it were the kind called punk; that they might
catch and retain some heavenly spark. I dwell as much
aloof from society as ever: find it just as impossible to
agree in opinion with the most intelligent of my neighbors; they not having improved one jot, nor I either. I
am still immersed in nature, have much of the time a
living sense of the breadth of the field on whose verge
I dwell."

That autumn, Marcus Spring, the philanthropic pa-
tron of Eagleswood near Perth Amboy, invited Thoreau,
at Alcott's suggestion, to survey the two hundred acres
and lecture at the same time. Eagleswood was primarily
a school for young people; Spring wanted to prepare
young people for maturity in a home-like environment
which included brilliant conversationalists and a leaven-
ing of Abolitionists. The school at Eagleswood was run
by Theodore Weld, and included, among others, Caroline
Kirkland, a Western story writer. Thoreau went, surveyed, conversed, lectured.

But he was his customary prickly self, which is to say
he made no concessions to his fellow lecturers or to his
students. He wrote his sister Sophia in November, "This
is a queer place—There is one large long stone building,
. . . in which I do not know exactly who or how many
work—. . . a few shops & offices, an old farm house and
Mr. Spring's perfectly private residence within 20 rods of
the main building. 'The City of Perth Amboy' is about
as big as Concord, and Eagleswood is 1¼ miles S W of it,
on the bay side. . . . Saturday evening I went to the
school room, hall, or what not, to see the children &
their teachers & patrons dance. Mr. Weld, a kind looking
man with a long white beard, danced with them, & Mr.

Cutler his assistant, lately from Cambridge, who is acquainted with Sanborn, Mr. Spring—and others. This Sat. eve-dance is a regular thing . . . They take it for granted that you want *society!*"

Not that Thoreau had any objection to dancing. He danced himself, especially in a pixielike mood on occasion at Ricketson's shanty when he deliberately trod on Alcott's toes. For the children of Concord he improvised dances, played his flute, popped corn, played juggler tricks, made willow whistles and trumpets out of squash leaf stems, and sang his favorite songs—*Canadian Boat Song, Tom Bowling* ("Here a sheer hulk lies poor Tom Bowling, / The darling of our crew; / No more he'll hear the tempest howling, / For death has broached him to.").

"On Sunday evening," he went on in his letter to Sophia, "I read the moose-story to the children to their satisfaction. Ever since I have been constantly engaged in surveying Eagleswood—through woods, ravines, marshes & along the shore, dodging the tide—through cat-briar mud & beggar ticks—having no time to look up or think where I am . . ." He wrote Blake with more appreciation of the lectures that he had given "with rare success" that he was "aware that what I was saying was silently taken in by their ears."

Of more importance, perhaps, was the fact that through Alcott's visits, Thoreau got into New York. Alcott took him to spend a day with Alice Cary, the poet, at Greeley's farm. They heard Henry Ward Beecher preach what Thoreau thought was rather a "pagan" sermon, and finally, a day or two later, they went to call on a man as independent and individual as Thoreau—Walt Whitman, whose *Leaves of Grass*—hailed by Emerson— had been published in 1855. Both Thoreau and Whitman were reserved, as if each feared to commit himself

152

too readily, but it was not the reserve of hostility, rather of uncertainty.

Whitman in his red-flannel undershirt, overalls, and calico jacket impressed Thoreau, an impression that grew after Thoreau returned to Eagleswood, for he wrote Blake of the meeting and Whitman—"He is apparently the greatest democrat the world has seen. Kings and aristocracy go by the board at once, as they have long deserved to. A remarkably strong though coarse nature, of a sweet disposition, and much prized by his friends. Though peculiar and rough in his exterior, . . . he is essentially a gentleman. I am still somewhat in a quandary about him,—feel that he is essentially strange to me, at any rate   "

He added, some weeks later, "That Walt Whitman . . . is the most interesting fact to me at present. I have just read his 2nd edition (which he gave me) and it has done me more good than any reading for a long time. Perhaps I remember best the poem of Walt Whitman an American & the Sun Down Poem. . . . But . . . he has spoken more truth than any American or modern that I know. . . . Of course Walt Whitman can communicate to us no experience, and if we are shocked, whose experience is it that we are reminded of? . . .

"We ought to rejoice greatly in him. He occasionally suggests something a little more than human. . . . He is awfully good. . . .

"Since I have seen him, I find that I am not disturbed by any brag or egoism in his book. He may turn out the least of a braggart of all, having a better right to be confident.

"He is a great fellow."

He returned to Concord from Eagleswood in a little over a month, as the year was drawing to its close. A long, friendly letter from Cholmondeley came to hand, but Thoreau must have wondered just how well Cholmondeley understood him after all when his British correspondent could write, "You are not living altogether as I could wish. You ought to have society. A college, a conventual life is for you. You should be the member of some society not yet formed. You want it greatly, and without this you will be liable to moulder away as you get older. . . . Your love for, and intimate acquaintance with, Nature is ancillary to some affection which you have not yet discovered."

On the last day of 1856, Thoreau, faithful to his ideal of existence, wrote to Blake in response to another invitation to lecture in Worcester before the winter was out, "O solitude! obscurity! meanness! I never triumph so as when I have the least success in my neighbor's eyes. The lecturer gets fifty dollars a night; but what becomes of his winter? What consolation will it be hereafter to have fifty thousand dollars for living in the world? I should like not to exchange *any* of my life for money."

CHAPTER 10

The Language of the Fields

> *Still we live meanly, like ants; though the fable*
> *tells us that we were long ago changed into men;*
> *like pygmies we fight with cranes; it is error upon*
> *error, and clout upon clout, and our best virtue has*
> *for its occasion a superfluous and evitable wretched-*
> *ness. Our life is frittered away by detail. An honest*
> *man has hardly need to count more than his ten*
> *fingers, or in extreme cases he may add his ten toes,*
> *and lump the rest. Simplicity, simplicity, simplicity!*
> *I say, let your affairs be as two or three, and not a*
> *hundred or a thousand; instead of a million count*
> *half a dozen, and keep your accounts on your*
> *thumb-nail.* —WALDEN

"How I love the simple, reserved country-men, my neighbors, who mind their own business and let me alone," wrote Thoreau in his journal late in 1856, "who never waylaid nor shot at me, to my knowledge, when I crossed their fields, though each one has a gun in his house! For nearly twoscore years I have known, at a distance, these long suffering men, whom I never spoke to, who never spoke to me, and now feel a certain tenderness for them, as if this long probation were but the prelude to an eternal friendship. What a long trial we have withstood, and how much more ad-mirable we are to each other, perchance, than if we had been bedfellows! I am not only grateful because Veias, and Homer, and Christ, and Shakespeare have lived, but

155

I am grateful for Minott, and Rice, and Melvin, and Goodwin, and Puffer even."

At his accustomed rounds, Thoreau met these countrymen with more ease than he met the audiences to which he lectured. Yet he continued to lecture. He promised Blake that he would lecture again in Worcester in February, once more on *Walking,* but a month before that occurrence he wrote in his journal: "For some years past I have partially offered myself as a lecturer; have been advertised as such several years. Yet I have had but two or three invitations to lecture in a year, and some years none at all. I congratulate myself on having been permitted to stay at home thus, I am so much richer for it. I do not see what I should have got of much value, but money, by going about, but I do see what I should have lost."

Despite a certain coolness which had come between Thoreau and the Emerson household, he was still on occasion dining there, to meet and talk about turtles with Agassiz, or to explore Eddy Emerson's snow cave— "a hole about two and a half feet wide and six feet long, into a drift, a little winding . . . I observed, as I approached in a course at right angles with the length of the cave, that the mouth of the cave was lit as if the light were close to it, so that I did not suspect its depth. Indeed, the light of this lamp was remarkably reflected and distributed. . . . I think that one lamp would light sufficiently a hall built of this material. . . . We afterward buried the lamp in a little crypt in this snowdrift and walled it in, and found that its light was visible, even in this *twilight,* through fifteen inches' thickness of snow."

Before going to Worcester, Thoreau lectured in Fitchburg. He had lectured in Amherst, New Hampshire, in

December, taken a month's freedom from lectures, and then in February delivered *Walking* at Fitchburg and Worcester. "Sometimes," he wrote after the Fitchburg lecture, "when, in conversation or a lecture, I have been grasping at, or even standing and reclining upon, the serene and everlasting truths that underlie and support our vacillating life, I have seen my auditors standing on their *terra firma*, the quaking earth, . . . and compassionately or timidly watching my motions as if they were the antics of a rope-dancer or mountebank pretending to walk on air . . ."

Thoreau was becoming more aware of the need for conservation of the nation's natural resources. It could hardly have been otherwise with so observant a walker. In his decades of tramping through the countryside he had witnessed the decline in numbers of the wild pigeons, the danger to fish in industrial growth along the rivers, the wanton felling of woodlands and even of old trees in Concord itself. His journal reflected his distress at the loss of familiar trees. "Every larger tree which I knew and admired is being gradually culled out and carried to mill. I see one or two more large oaks in Hubbard's woods lying high on stumps, waiting for snow to be removed. I miss them as surely and with the same feeling that I do the old inhabitants out of the village street." But he was also aware that there was little he could do about it. "No doubt there is *some* compensation for this loss, but I do not at this moment see clearly what it is."

In February, Sanborn brought a Concord visitor to lunch at the Thoreau house. This was John Brown, already widely known throughout the east because he was the leader of the anti-slavery forces in Kansas, which was ever since the opening of Kansas to settlement in

1855 a battleground between pro-slavery and anti-slavery groups. Brown himself had led violent raids and participated in the Pottawatomie massacre of pro-slavery colonists near Dutch Henry's Crossing at Pottawatomie Creek. He was now touring the east in an effort to raise funds for the cause against slavery. Sanborn had persuaded him to come to Concord to meet some of the leading citizens. Emerson joined them at Thoreaus' and they talked with Brown. At Thoreaus' Brown spoke passionately but quietly of liberty and the rights of all men, black as well as white, and told his listeners something of his history.

At the Town House that night, speaking to the people who had come to hear him, something of the violence in him burst forth when he spoke wildly and bitterly, with many gestures, of the way his son John had been treated in Kansas. He talked about his trials—with one son murdered, another crazed, and told his listeners in ringing words that he and his remaining sons would never stop fighting to free Kansas from slavery. And next day at Emerson's he held forth again, gentler now, entertaining young Eddy with animal stories.

Thoreau was impressed by him and made a donation. So did many others, including Emerson. But of them all, Thoreau's impression of Brown went deepest, and it was to show through later.

Meanwhile, Thoreau's excursions to Walden, Fair Haven, up the Assabet, to Conantum, Hubbard's Close and all the old places continued unabated. But he was planning excursions farther afield in 1857. Though he wrote to Ricketson April first that he wished "there were a few more signs of spring in myself—however, I take it that there *are* as many within us as we think we hear *without* us. I am decent for steady pace, but not yet for a race."—he followed the letter to New Bedford. There he, Alcott, Channing and Ricketson had many lively conversations, but, as usual, he was often alone, by choice. He "caught a croaking frog in some smooth water," studied frog spawn ("in very handsome spherical masses of transparent jelly . . . suspended near the surface of some weed"), visited the New Bedford Library, gathered bayberries, picked up scallop shells, watched the smelt fishermen, spent a rainy day in Ricketson's shanty, and visited the Marlborough ponds at long last.

He set out to walk around Little Quitticus, and outwalked Ricketson ("the water being high,—higher than anciently even, on account of dams, we had to go round the swamp at the south end . . . and R. gave it up. I went to Long Pond and waited for him . . ."). While waiting for his host, Thoreau examined the turtles in the area and made notes on the back of a lottery circular. Another day of rain followed—a day of conversation in the shanty, no doubt.

On April 16 he was back in Concord, getting birch sap, and telling Sanborn how, a month previous, he had been needled in the post-office by Abel Brooks about his "walkers" society. Sanborn told him that when first he had come to Concord and boarded at Holbrook's, he had asked Holbrook how many religious societies there were in town. Holbrook had told him there were three—"the Unitarian, the Orthodox, and the Walden Pond Society. I asked Sanborn with which Holbrook classed himself. He said he believes that he put himself with the last."

He resumed his walks about Concord, but he also spent much time in his boat, rowing up the Assabet and sailing to Ball's Hill. He made notes on lichens and mosses, and was distressed at sight of a dead snake ("I have the same objection to killing a snake that I have to

159

the killing of any other animal, yet the most humane man that I know never omits to kill one."). He heard the first toad song and built a fence as well as an arbor for Emerson. He added to his modest wardrobe—

"Within a week I have had made a pair of corduroy pants, which cost when done $1.60. They are of that peculiar clay-color, reflecting the light from portions of their surface. They have this advantage, that, beside being very strong, they will look about as well three months hence as now,—or as ill, some would say. Most of my friends are disturbed by my wearing them. I can get four or five pairs for what one ordinary pair would cost in Boston, and each of the former will last two or three times as long under the same circumstances. The tailor said that the stuff was not made in this country; that it was worn by the Irish at home, and now they would not look at it, but others would not wear it, durable and cheap as it is, because it is worn by the Irish. Moreover, I like the color on other accounts. Anything but black clothes."

Late in May Ricketson returned his visit. Thoreau took him by boat to Fair Haven, where they bathed, finding "the water unexpectedly warm and the air also delicious. Thus we are baptized into nature." Ricketson, however, never stayed long; he was apparently too restless to stay in one place, other than his shanty, very long.

On June 12, 1857, Thoreau set out for Cape Cod. He went alone this time. As usual, he made copious notes. Perhaps he intended to add to his store of writing about Cape Cod, but nothing of this excursion was subsequently used either on the lecture platform or in print. At Clark's Island, B. M. Watson told Thoreau solemnly that Daniel Webster once saw "the sea-serpent . . . with a head somewhat like a horse's raised some six feet above

160

the water, and his body the size of a cask trailing behind. He was careering over the bay, chasing the mackerel. . . . On the sail homeward, Webster having had time to reflect on what had occurred, at length said to Peterson, 'For God's sake, never say a word about this to any one, for if it should be known that I have seen the sea-serpent, I should never hear the last of it, but wherever I went should have to tell the story to every one I met.' So it has not leaked out till now."

After a ride to Manomet with Watson and his wife, Thoreau started off by himself, shouldering his pack to walk along the shore. He went along taking note of the vegetation, listening to the booming of a bittern ("I heard distinctly two or three dry, hard sucks, as if the bird were drawing up water from the swamp, and then the sounds usually heard, as if ejecting it"), watching laying turtles, and, after walking seven miles that day, spent the night at the house of one Samuel Ellis. The Ellises were accustomed to taking in pedlars, which they thought Thoreau to be—as Ricketson had once thought him, too, which conveys the undeniable impression that —on his excursions at least—Thoreau wore the general appearance of a pedlar. There he made the acquaintance of a genuine pedlar who arrived after him with a horse and cart, "a simple and well-behaved boy of sixteen or seventeen only, peddling cutlery, who said that he started from Conway . . . In answer to my question how he liked peddling, he said that he liked it on some accounts, it enabled him to see the world. I thought him an unusually good specimen of Young America."

Next day he set out again, after listening to his host's morning prayers thanking God "that we 'of all the pale-faces were preserved alive,' " and musing—"What's the use of ushering the day with prayer, if it is . . . con-

161

secrated to turning a few more pennies merely?" He walked along a sandy road half a mile from the Atlantic, observing the snake rail fences, met and talked with an Indian, watched the "piping plover," and skipping beach-flies. At Scusset he took the train to Sandwich.

Once again out of "the cars," he went on his way with chart and compass by means of which he could "generally find a shorter way than the inhabitants can tell me." He went on to Friends Village, "a continuous street, for five miles at least, without a distinct village, the houses but a few rods apart all the way on each side. . . . As in Canada along the St. Lawrence, you never got out of the village, only came to a meeting-house now and then. . . . But all this street had a peculiarly Sabbath-day appearance, for there was scarcely an inhabitant to be seen, and they were commonly women or young children, for the greater part of the able-bodied men were gone to sea . . ."

He recorded his despondency at walking in settled regions, "but when I come out upon a bare and solitary heath am at once exhilarated. This is a common experience in my travelling. I plod along, thinking what a miserable world this is and what miserable fellows we that inhabit it, wondering what it is tempts men to live in it; but anon I leave the towns behind and am lost in some boundless heath, and life becomes gradually more tolerable, if not even glorious." He walked to the ponds between Harwich and Brewster where he "met with the first cranberry-patch . . . a handsome, perfectly level bed, a field, a redeemed meadow, adjoining the pond, the plants in perfectly straight rows eighteen inches apart, in coarse white sand which had been carted in."

He walked through mizzling rain and fog to Truro.

On the way he picked up a Mother Carey's chicken, washed up dead on the beach, and carried it along, "tied to the tip of my umbrella, dangling outside. When the inhabitants saw me come up from the beach this stormy day, with this emblem dangling from my umbrella, and saw me set it up in a corner carefully to be out of the way of cats, they may have taken me for a crazy man." This must have afforded Thoreau some amusement; he did not mind being taken for what he was or what he was not, as long as people did not take him for what they thought he ought to be.

The fog held for five days, but Thoreau was out in it, nothing daunted, though some of the Cape dwellers "denied that it was fog at all. They said with some asperity that it was rain. Yet more rain would have fallen in a smart shower in the country in twenty minutes than in these five days on the Cape." When the fog cleared, Thoreau went to Provincetown, "straight across the country to the Bay where the new road strikes it, directly through the pine plantation," and spent the night in an attic chamber at the Pilgrim House ("It would be worth the while to send a professor there, one who was also skilled in entomology.") He added, as he put it, considerable "to my knowledge of the natural history of the rat and the bedbug. . . . At still midnight, when, half awake, half asleep, you seem to be weltering in your own blood on a battlefield, you hear the stealthy tread of padded feet belonging to some animal of the cat tribe, perambulating the roof within a few inches of your head."

He reached home late in the afternoon of June 22nd, and was soon out at Farmer's Owl-Nest Swamp looking for a long-eared owl's nest near the top of a white pine, thirty feet from the ground. Thoreau climbed the tree to

163

look at it, untroubled by the distress of the owl; the nest was empty. "It was made of twigs rather less than an eighth of an inch thick and was almost flat above, only an inch lower in the middle than at the edge, about sixteen inches in diameter and six or eight inches thick, with the twigs in the midst, and beneath was mixed sphagnum and sedge from the swamp beneath, and the lining or flooring was coarse strips of grape-vine bark; the whole pretty firmly matted together. How common and important a material is grape-vine bark for birds' nests! Nature wastes nothing."

A fortnight after he had resumed his accustomed rounds and spent a day on the Assabet with Blake, he recorded a footnote on Cape Cod. "Some of the inhabitants of the Cape," he wrote July 7, "think that the Cape is theirs and all occupied by them, but in my eyes it is no more theirs than it is the blackbirds', and in visiting the Cape there is hardly more need of my regarding or going through the villages than of going through the blackbirds' nests. I am inclined to leave them both on one side, or perchance I just glance into them to see how they are built and what they contain. I know that they have *spoken for* the whole Cape, and lines are drawn on their maps accordingly, but I know that these are imaginary, having perambulated many such, and they would have to get me or one of my craft to find them for them. For the most part, indeed with very trifling exceptions, there were no human beings there, only a few imaginary lines on a map."

Next day he wrote to Calvin Greene that he had not published anything for some time, but his pen was not idle. "I like a private life, & cannot bear to have the public in my mind." He wrote also that he was "very little of a traveller," and in the sense that Thoreau

164

meant it this was true, for he had reference to an extended Western trip. But he was even then thinking of yet another trip into the Maine woods. He asked his cousin in Bangor, George Thatcher, to accompany him. George could not do so. Thoreau then turned to Edward Hoar—that same companion with whom Thoreau had accidentally set fire to the Concord woods thirteen years before. On July 20th, they set out for Maine to engage a guide and plunge once more into the wilderness.

Their guide was an Indian, Joe Polis ("stoutly built, perhaps a little above the middle height, with a broad face, and . . . perfect Indian features and complexion"). Polis proved to be well informed in the very subjects Thoreau wanted to study in preparation for the book on Indian life he planned to write but never wrote. Polis, a Penobscot, knew the country into which they planned to go—up to the Allegash Lakes by way of Moosehead—and persuaded them to return not by the route they had originally chosen, but by the East Branch of the Penobscot River, since it led through wilder country.

They set out from Bangor in rain which stayed with them for miles. Thoreau and Hoar each carried a large knapsack, "as full as it would hold," with provisions and utensils in two large India-rubber bags. Polis had only an axe, a gun, a blanket, tobacco and a pipe. Thoreau observed the impressive simplicity of the Indian's equipment. It was still raining when they reached Moosehead Lake on the evening of July 23d; so they stayed in a tavern that night and launched the canoe into the lake next morning, at four o'clock. The canoe was more compact than Thoreau had thought it might be, but it was new and staunch, and carried the six hundred pounds of travelers and baggage without difficulty. Off they went, the Indian "on a cross-bar in the stern, but we flat on the bottom . . . and one of us commonly paddled with the Indian."

Thoreau, as usual, made copious notes, adding to his lists of trees, shrubs and flowers. But he was as much interested in what Joe Polis did and what the Indian could tell him of Indian life and lore as he was in the wilderness through which they passed. His notes are studded with Indian words and their meanings—"*Allegash,* hemlock-bark. . . . *Penobscot,* Rocky River. *Puapeskou,* stone. . . . *Sebago* or *Sebec,* large open water." Polis sang for them in "a slow, somewhat nasal, yet musical chant, in his own language. . . . His singing carried me back to the period of the discovery of America, to San Salvador and the Incas, when Europeans first encountered the simple faith of the Indian. There was, indeed, a beautiful simplicity about it; nothing of the dark and savage, only the mild and infantile."

The Indian constantly surprised his employers. On their first night in camp he announced that a sound he heard was made by a snake. "He imitated it at my request," Thoreau noted, "making a low whistling note,—*pheet—pheet,*—two or three times repeated, somewhat like the peep of the hylodes, but not so loud. In answer to my inquiries, he said that he had never seen them while making it, but going to the spot he finds the snake."

Thoreau plied Polis with questions. Even such a natural phenomenon as phosphorescent wood which Thoreau found that first night—a find which Thoreau felt "paid for" his journey—is set down in its Indian name, *Artoosoqu'.* Polis fascinated Thoreau by the variety of experiences he or "his folks" before him had had. "Nature must have made a thousand revelations to them which are still secrets to us," observed Thoreau. He was

166

somewhat surprised next day to be chided by Polis because he confessed, in answer to an inquiry from the Indian, that he did not go to church on Sunday, but sat in his chamber reading in the morning and went to walk in the afternoon. And he must have been taken aback when, in response to a question about how he did something, Polis replied, "Oh, I can't tell *you*. Great difference between me and white man."

Thoreau's account of this last trip to the Maine woods is filled with the customary observations about a great variety of things—the note of the white-throated sparrow ("a very inspiriting but almost wiry sound"), the Creeping Snowberry ("It had a slight checkerberry flavor . . ."), the larch woods ("tall and slender trees with fantastic branches"), the great purple-fringed orchis ("It is remarkable that such delicate flowers should here adorn these wilderness paths."), the No-see-ems ("the little midge . . . *Simulium nocivum* . . . a kind of sand-fly. . . . They are said to get under your clothes, and produce a feverish heat . . ."), the voice of the loon ("a very wild sound, quite in keeping with the place and the circumstances of the traveler, and very unlike the voice of a bird. I could lie awake for hours listening to it, it is so thrilling."), the portages ("a tangled and perplexing thicket, through which we stumbled and threaded our way")—but the account of the excursion is primarily an account of a trip with an Indian, what he did, what he said, what he thought. Thoreau learned more from Joe Polis about the way in which human beings adapted to a wilderness environment than he did of nature on this journey.

Thoreau reached home early in the morning of August 8th, and found half a dozen glow-worms, sent by B. M. Watson from Plymouth, waiting for his examination. He wrote Watson that two of them remained just about as bright as at first. "It was a singular coincidence that I should find these worms awaiting me, for my mind was full of a phosphoresence which I had seen in the woods." He fell readily into his customary pattern, but delayed answering most of his mail for ten or twelve days.

To Blake he wrote on August 18th about his Maine excursion, "I have had a quite profitable journey, chiefly from associating with an intelligent Indian. . . . Having returned, I flatter myself that the world appears in some respects a little larger, and not, as usual, smaller and shallower, for having extended my range. I have made a short excursion into the new world which the Indian dwells in, or *is*. He begins where we leave off. It is worth the while to detect new faculties in man,—he is so much the more divine; and anything that fairly excites our admiration expands us. The Indian, who can find his way so wonderfully in the woods, possesses so much intelligence which the white man does not,—and it increases my own capacity, as well as faith, to observe it. I rejoice to find that intelligence flows in other channels than I knew. It redeems for me portions of what seemed brutish before.

"It is a great satisfaction to find that your oldest convictions are permanent. With regard to essentials, I have never had occasion to change my mind. The aspect of the world varies from year to year, as the landscape is differently clothed, but I find that the *truth* is still *true* . . . ." Truth as much as freedom was still Thoreau's grail.

To Ricketson he wrote on the same day the sparest of accounts of his two trips—to Cape Cod and the Maine woods—and at length about Wilson Flagg's *Studies in the Field & Forest* ("he is not alert enough. He wants stirring up with a pole."), and struck off some pointed lines on literary style.

"As for style of writing—if one has any thing to say, it drops from him simply & directly, as a stone falls to the ground, for there are no two ways about it, but down it comes, and he may stick in the points and stops whenever he can get a chance. New ideas come into this world somewhat like falling meteors, with a flash and an explosion, and perhaps somebody's castle roof perforated. To try to polish the stone in its descent, to give it a peculiar turn and make it whistle a tune perchance, would be of no use, if it were possible. Your polished stuff turns out not to be meteoric, but of this earth.— However there is plenty of time, and Nature is an admirable schoolmistress."

His excursions behind him, Thoreau spent the remainder of that year at home, declining invitations to visit anywhere. His father was ill—"quite sick with the jaundice . . . this, added to his long standing cold, has reduced him very much," and it was upon Thoreau that the work of the graphite business now devolved. The business may have diminished somewhat temporarily because of the panic of 1857, but it was probably not much affected by it.

Yet Thoreau took notice of the panic. It was unusual for him to pay much attention to what went on very far from Concord, except in the domain of ideas. He wrote Blake in mid-November what amounted to a lecture on hard times. "They make a great ado nowadays about hard times. . . . It is not enough to be industrious; so are the ants. What are you industrious about? . . . The merchants and company have long laughed at transcendentalism, higher laws, etc., crying, 'None of your moonshine,' as if they were anchored to something not only definite, but sure and permanent. . . . But there is the moonshine still, serene, beneficent, and unchanged."

He went on excursions about Concord with redoubled energy. This was only to be expected. When the graphite business made greater demands upon his time, he was all the more eager to be up and about his real business, as chronicler of the wild in man and nature and inspector of that corner of the world which he had made so intimately his own. He resented visitors who kept him from his walks. He chafed at them in his journal, October 7th, when he wrote, "I do not know how to entertain one who can't take long walks. The first thing that suggests itself is to get a horse to draw them, and that brings us at once into contact with stablers and dirty harness, and I do not get over my ride for a long time. I give up my forenoon to them and get along pretty well, the very elasticity of the air and promise of the day abetting me, but they are as heavy as dumplings by mid-afternoon. If they can't walk, why won't they take an honest nap and let me go in the afternoon? But, come two o'clock, they alarm me by an evident disposition to sit. In the midst of the most glorious Indian-summer afternoon, there they sit, breaking your chairs and wearing out the house, with their backs to the light, taking no note of the lapse of time."

But a month later, when he wrote to Blake, he was indignant at the idea that he should listen to lectures. Dr. Reinhold Solger was lecturing in Concord, to Sanborn's students. Emerson and Alcott had listened to Dr. Solger on the subject of geography, and Emerson asked Thoreau if he, too, would not go to listen to the speaker. "What," he wrote Blake, "to be sitting in a meeting-house cellar at that time of day, when you might possibly be out-doors! I never thought of such a thing. What was the sun made for? If he does not prize daylight, I do. Let him lecture to owls and dormice. He must be a wonderful lecturer indeed who can keep me indoors at such an hour, when the night is coming in which no man can walk."

He was happy to be home, and all his life consistent in this. His journal was the repository for his convictions about his relation to his home place. Late in November he set down lines which were profoundly true for him, as they are true for thousands of other men and women less articulate than Thoreau. "A man is worth most to himself and to others, whether as an observer, or poet, or neighbor, or friend, where he is most himself, most contented and at home. There his life is the most intense and he loses the fewest moments. Familiar and surrounding objects are the best symbols and illustrations of his life. . . . The poet has made the best roots in his native soil of any man, and is the hardest to transplant. The man who is often thinking that it is better to be somewhere else than where he is excommunicates himself. If a man is rich and strong anywhere, it must be on his native soil. Here I have been these forty years learning the language of these fields that I may the better express myself."

CHAPTER 11

"Conformity Is Death"

> *We talk about a representative government; but what a monster of a government is that where the noblest faculties of the mind, and the whole heart, are not represented. A semi-human tiger or ox, stalking over the earth, with its heart taken out and the top of its brain shot away. . . .*
>
> *The only government that I recognize—and it matters not how few are at the head of it, or how small its army—is that power that establishes justice in the land, never that which establishes injustice.*
>
> —A PLEA FOR CAPTAIN JOHN BROWN

IT was true, as Thoreau had written his correspondents, that he had not recently published very much. In this respect, however, 1858 opened auspiciously for him. A new magazine had begun publication in Boston in 1857, and its editor, James Russell Lowell, asked for something from Thoreau—either directly, or through Emerson. Thoreau wrote Lowell late in January that he had been busy surveying, and had scarcely "had time to 'think' of your proposition." But he was not inclined to send in the account he had written of the most recent expedition to Maine because Joe Polis could read, and Thoreau reported his words and deeds too faithfully; "I could not face him again." He sent him instead his account of the second expedition, *Chesuncook*. Lowell accepted it and scheduled it for the June and July issues of *The Atlantic Monthly*.

It seems to have been Thoreau's pattern as a writer to be solicited for material; he put his work on offer very seldom, and Horace Greeley's activity on behalf of Thoreau's work exceeded his own. Clearly, he considered that his primary business was still keeping the accounts of Concord—the records of its wood life, the annals of its meadows, ponds, rivers; publication was secondary. His income from the graphite business and his occasional lectures was evidently enough to satisfy his small needs, and such income as he might gain from publication must not have seemed to Thoreau worth the effort of putting himself out to get it.

The records he kept, such as survive, were meticulous. When Thomas Wentworth Higginson wrote him in January, 1858, to ask about the possibility of going to Quebec by way of the Allegash, Thoreau could give an account of his journey ("We went about 325 miles with the canoe [including 60 miles of Stage between Bangor & Oldtown] were out 12 nights, & spent about 40 dollars apiece, which was more than was necessary. We paid the Indian, who was a very good one, $1.50 per day & 50 cts. per week for his canoe.") and of his needs on the excursion that was as detailed as anyone could wish ("We *used* [3 of us] exactly 26 lbs. of hard bread, 14 lbs. of pork, 3 lbs. of coffee, 12 lbs. of sugar [& could have used more] besides a little tea, Ind. meal, & rice & plenty of berries & moosemeat. This was faring very luxuriously. I had not formerly carried coffee—sugar, or rice. But for solid food, I decide that *it is not worth the while to carry anything but hard bread & pork,* whatever your tastes & habits may be. These wear best—& you have no time nor dishes in which to cook any thing else. Of course you will take a little Ind. meal to fry fish in—& half a dozen lemons also, if you have sugar—will be very refreshing—for the

water is warm. . . . Don't forget an India rubber knapsack—with a large flap—plenty of *dish cloths*—old newspapers, strings, & 25 feet of strong cord."). To this and
more, Thoreau added that he "could be more particular,
but perhaps have been too much so already."

Perhaps because the panic of the preceding year made
the demand for graphite lessen a little, Thoreau was
abroad very often, both at surveying and at his walks
through the neighborhood. His entries in his journal for
that year were at length and much varied. He had his
lichen days, his frog days, his turtle days—days on which
he was particularly aware of or interested in certain
phenomena of nature. He was as likely to start off from
lichens into philosophical asides about his fellowmen
("How protean is life! One may eat and drink and sleep
and digest, and do the ordinary duties of a man, and
have no excuse for sending for a doctor, and yet he may
have reason to doubt if he is as truly alive or his life is
as valuable and divine as that of an oyster. He may be
the very best citizen in the town, and yet it shall occur
to him to prick himself with a pin to see if he is alive.
It is wonderful how quiet, harmless, and ineffective a
living creature may be. No more energy may it have than
a fungus that lifts the bark of a decaying tree. I raised
last summer a squash which weighed 123½ pounds. If
it had fallen on me it would have made as deep and
lasting an impression as most men do.") as he was to
learn, by dint of cutting holes in the ice at Gowing's
Swamp that "sphagnum will grow on the surface of water
five feet deep!"

That winter being open, deep snow did not limit
Thoreau's hikes nor impede his surveying. He observed
"that herbaceous plants show less greenness than usual
. . . , having been more exposed for want of a snowy

covering" and that tea made of spruce was "in spite of a slight piny or turpentine flavor . . . unexpectedly good." He was ever the inquirer, not in a narrowly scientific sense, but rather in that of the naturalist. He observed, he appreciated, he chronicled, he probed and learned, but his goal was not fundamentally scientific.

He was interested in tree rings ("in that oak stump on the ditch-bank by Trillium Wood . . . between the twentieth and twenty-seventh rings there was only about three-sevenths of an inch, though before and after this it grew very fast and seven spaces would make nearly two inches. The tree was growing lustily till twenty years old, and then for seven years it grew only one fourth or one fifth part as fast as before and after. I am curious to know what happened."), in the entrances to burrows ("Those small holes in the ground,—musquash, mice, etc.,—thickly beset with crystals of frost, remind me of the invisible vapor issuing thence which may be called Earth's breath, though you might think it were the breath of a mouse."), in snow buntings ("They are trotting about briskly over the snow amid the weeds,—apparently pigweed and Roman wormwood,—as it were to keep their toes warm, hopping up to the weeds. Then they restlessly take to wing again, and as they wheel about one, it is a very rich sight to see them dressed in black and white uniforms, alternate black and white, very distinct and regular."), in a Chippewa Indian who came to speak in Concord early in March and whom he plied with questions, in the language of the Indians ("It reveals to me a life within a life, or rather a life without a life, as it were threading the woods between our towns still, and yet we can never tread in its trail. The Indian's earthly life was as far off from us as heaven is."), in the cry of a flicker ("how that single sound peoples and enriches all the woods and fields!"), in the view from Fair Haven Hill ("I think that Concord affords no better view. It is always incredibly fair, but ordinarily we are mere objects in it, and not witnesses of it. I see . . . a valley extending southwest and northeast and some two miles across, . . . with a broad, yellow meadow tinged with brown at the bottom, and a blue river winding slowly through it northward, with a regular edging of low bushes on the brink, of the same color with the meadow. . . . Such is the dwelling-place of man; but go to the caucus in the village to-night or to a church to-morrow, and see if there is anything said to suggest that the inhabitants of those houses know what kind of world they live in.").

That spring Thoreau corrected proofs of *Chesuncook,* and the first part of that account appeared in the June issue of *The Atlantic Monthly.* In June Thoreau climbed Monadnock, which reared almost four thousand feet northwest of Concord; Blake accompanied him. They carried packs on their backs and mounted to the summit to watch the sun set, though they lost their way coming back down ("nothing is easier than to lose your way here, where so little trail is left upon the rocks"). Thoreau was struck by the insistence of hikers in carving names into the rocks. "These sculptors seemed to me to court such alliance with the grave as they who put their names over tombstones along the highway. . . . Apparently a part of the regular outfit of mountain-climbers is a hammer and cold-chisel, . . . Certainly you could not hire a stone-cutter to do so much engraving for less than several thousand dollars. But no Old Mortality will ever be caught renewing these epitaphs. It reminds what kind of steeps do climb the false pretenders to fame, whose chief exploit is the carriage of the tools with which to inscribe their names. For speaking epitaphs they are,

176

and the mere name is a sufficient revelation of the character. They are all of one trade,—stone-cutters, defacers of mountain-tops. 'Charles & Lizzie!' Charles carried the sledge-hammer, and Lizzie the cold-chisel. Some have carried up a paint-pot, and painted their names on the rocks."

They spent all the next day there, Thoreau industriously setting down the names of all the plants growing on the heights, and the two of them exploring the mountain. "But the most interesting part of this walk," he wrote, on the way back to Concord next day, "was the three miles along the railroad between State Line and Winchendon Station. . . . The railroad runs very straight for long distances here through a primitive forest." By June fifth, Thoreau was once again surveying in the northeast part of Lincoln.

Later that month the July issue of *The Atlantic Monthly* carrying the second part of *Chesuncook* came out. Much to his anger, Thoreau discovered that his proofs had once again been tampered with by an editor. James Russell Lowell, who lived in a more social and academic milieu than Thoreau did, and who was far more sensitive to the opinions of the public than Thoreau could be, deleted one pantheistic sentence which would certainly have disturbed some men of the cloth who might have read Thoreau's account of his excursion. On June 22, Thoreau wrote him a cold, stiff letter of protest—

"When I received the proof of that portion of my story printed in the May number of your magazine, I was surprised to find that the sentence—'It is as immortal as I am, and perchance will go to as high a heaven, there to tower above me still.'—(which comes directly after the words 'heal my cuts,' page 230, tenth line from

177

the top,) had been crossed out, and it occurred to me that, after all, it was of some consequence that I should see the proofs; supposing, of course, that my 'Stet' &c in the margin would be respected, as I perceive that it was in other cases of comparatively little importance to me. However, I have just noticed that that sentence was, in a very mean and cowardly manner, omitted. I hardly need to say that this is a liberty which I will not permit to be taken with my MS. The editor has, in this case, no more right to omit a sentiment than to insert one, or put words into my mouth. I do not ask anybody to adopt my opinions, but I do expect that when they ask for them to print, they will print them, or obtain my consent to their alteration, or omission. I should not read many books if I thought that they had been thus expurgated. I feel this treatment to be an insult, though not intended as such, for it is to presume that I can be hired to suppress my opinions.

"I do not mean to charge you with this omission, for I cannot believe that you knew anything about it, but there must be a responsible editor somewhere, and you, to whom I entrusted my MS. are the only party that I know in this matter. I therefore write to ask if you sanction this omission, and if there are any other sentiments to be omitted in the remainder of my article. If you do not sanction it—or whether you do or not—will you do me the justice to print that sentence, as an omitted one, indicating its place, in the August number?

"I am not willing to be associated in any way, unnecessarily, with parties who will confess themselves so bigoted & timid as this implies. I could excuse a man who was afraid of an uplifted fist, but if one habitually manifests fear at the utterance of a sincere thought, I must think that his life is a kind of nightmare continued

178

into broad daylight. It is hard to conceive of one so completely derivative. Is this the avowed character of *The Atlantic Monthly?* I should like an early reply."

No record of Lowell's reply has been found. Presumably, therefore, no reply was made, for Thoreau's subsequent refusal to submit anything further to *The Atlantic Monthly* as long as Lowell remained its editor suggests that he heard nothing from Lowell, and that therefore Lowell condoned the deletion of the disputed sentence.

Having put himself on record unmistakably, Thoreau patently considered the episode finished. He busied himself with plans for an excursion to the White Mountains and asked Blake to accompany Edward Hoar and him self; a day later he proposed that Blake's friend, Theophilus Brown, also go along. Neither, however, found it possible to go immediately, but promised to join Thoreau later. Thoreau and Hoar went alone, starting the second day of July "in a private carriage,"—a horse and covered wagon Hoar had arranged for. They drove to Merrimack and stopped overnight at a tavern there. Thoreau, as was his custom, went out for an evening walk finding that "The wood thrush sings almost wherever I go, eternally reconsecrating the world, morning and evening, for us." He walked whenever he could do so en route ("You have to sacrifice so much to the horse. You cannot choose the most agreeable places in which to spend the noon, commanding the finest views, because commonly there is no water there, or you cannot get there with your horse.").

Their goal was Mount Washington, the highest point in New England. They reached the base of the mountain late on the fifth day of their excursion, hired a local man to help with their baggage, and began the ascent next day. On the second day of the ascent they reached the summit and camped there. They managed with the help of their guide, Wentworth—to set a spreading fire, which did not, however, approximate the damage done at Concord by Thoreau and Hoar. Here Blake and Brown finally joined them, and they slept five in the tent that night, while rain put out their fire.

On July 9th, Thoreau, continuing his exploration of the ravines, miscalculated a jump, and sprained his ankle. He spent a sleepless night, in consequence, and could not walk next day. That day of inactivity was one in which he was much troubled—as Blake and Brown had been on their ascent—by black flies ("They compelled me most of the time to sit in the smoke, which I preferred to wearing a veil. They lie along your forehead in a line, where your hat touches it, or behind your ears, or about your throat [if not protected by a beard], . . . and there suck till they are crushed. . . . Anything but mosquitoes by night.").

By the twelfth of July they had begun the descent of Mt. Washington; a week later Thoreau was back in Concord setting down a list of necessities for such an excursion—"Three strong check shirts. Two pairs socks. Neck ribbon and handkerchief. Three pocket-handkerchiefs. . . . A large, broad india-rubber knapsack, with a *broad* flap. . . . Pins, needles, thread. . . . A cap to lie in at night. . . . Veil and *gloves* (or enough millinet to cover all at night). . . . Botany, spyglass, microscope. Tape, insect-boxes. . . . Hard-bread (sweet crackers good); a moist, sweet plum cake very good and lasting; pork, corned beef or tongue, sugar, tea or coffee, and a little salt."

He was scarcely settled into his Concord routine once more before, at the time of the autumnal equinox, he was off to Cape Ann with Channing. He visited with his friends, the Russells, and on this excursion he and Channing spent some time in Marblehead, Salem and Rockport, where they walked for the most part and prepared their own meals, using, "as usual, dead bayberry bushes for fuel. . . . They make a very quick fire, and I noticed that their smoke covered our dippers with a kind of japan which did not crack or come off nearly so much as ordinary soot."

They stayed only four days. On September 25th he went "a-graping up Assabet with some young ladies." Perhaps he had mellowed a little since he wrote in his journal seven years before, on the occasion of a party at Emerson's, "I confess that I am lacking a sense, perchance, in this respect, and I derive no pleasure from talking with a young woman half an hour simply because she has regular features. The society of young women is the most unprofitable I have ever tried. They are so light and flighty that you can never be sure whether they are there or not there. I prefer to talk with the more staid and settled, *settled for life,* in every sense."

He went to work at a possible lecture on the subject of autumnal tints and wrote Ricketson to learn "how much our trees differ from English & European ones in this respect." Ricketson sent him the information he required, and asked him to visit again at New Bedford. But Thoreau would not leave Concord again at this time because his father was ill and did not appear to be mending. Cholmondeley, on his way from Canada to Jamaica, visited Thoreau early that December, but for the most part that autumn and winter Thoreau was writing, keeping his journal, and devoting ever more time to the business of manufacturing graphite since his father was too ill to work.

His friends made repeated efforts to draw Thoreau

into their company. He was invited to Emerson's, to "an Alcottian conversation," to meet Henry James ("a hearty man enough, with whom you can differ very satisfactorily, on account of both his doctrines and his good temper"). He went to a meeting of the Saturday Club at the Parker House; its members included Emerson, Longfellow, Holmes, Agassiz, Lowell, and other distinguished literary men. Thoreau "found it hard to see through the cigar smoke, and men were deposited about in chairs over the marble floor, as thick as legs of bacon in a smokehouse. It was all smoke, and no salt, Attic or other."

He wrote to Blake, "The doctors are all agreed that I am suffering from want of society. Was never a case like it. First, I did not know that I was suffering at all. Secondly, as an Irishman might say, I had thought it was indigestion of the society I got." His journal reflected his reaction. "All the community may scream," he wrote December 27, "because one man is born who will not do as it does, who will not conform because conformity to him is death,—he is so constituted. They know nothing about his case; they are fools when they presume to advise him. The man of genius knows what he is aiming at; nobody else knows. And he alone knows when something comes between him and his object. In the course of generations, however, men will excuse you for not doing as they do, if you will bring enough to pass in your own way."

Thoreau's father declined steadily in health. On January 13, 1859, he retired to his bedroom and did not come out of it again. His illness was now quite clearly terminal, and he died in mid-afternoon February third. Though Thoreau had made little mention of his father's illness in his journal, his entry for that date briefly sketched his father's history and added, "As far as I know, Father, when he died, was not only one of the oldest men

182

in the middle of Concord, but the one perhaps best acquainted with the inhabitants, and the local, social, and street history of the middle of the town, for the last fifty years. He belonged in a peculiar sense to the village street; loved to sit in the shops or at the post-office and read the daily papers." And, after a few paragraphs about the Indians, he added, "I perceive that we partially die ourselves through sympathy at the death of each of our friends or near relatives. Each such experience is an assault on our vital force. It becomes a source of wonder that they who have lost many friends still live. After long watching around the sick-bed of a friend, we, too, partially give up the ghost with him, and are the less to be identified with this state of things."

A few days later he answered a letter of sympathy from Ricketson ("I was much impressed with his good sense, his fine social nature, and genuine hospitality."), "I am glad to read what you say about his social nature. I think I may say that he was wholly unpretending; and there was this peculiarity in his aim, that, though he had pecuniary difficulties to contend with the greater part of his life, he always studied merely how to make a *good* article, pencil or other . . ."

Thoreau speedily resumed his way of life, watching the muskrat-hunters ("I meet these gods of the river and woods with sparkling faces   while the dull regular priests are steering their parish rafts in a prose mood"), and keeping the annals of Concord. The birds may not have sounded as sweet to him as before the death of his father, as he noted, but he was none the less given to attending their affairs. He gave another lecture, this time on *Autumnal Tints,* on February 22 at Worcester. And, the necessity of running the graphite business notwithstanding, he took a major job of surveying—this time measuring the water depths of the constantly flooding Concord, Sudbury, and Assabet Rivers, and set down the history of the bridges crossing them, and their abutments. He thought himself as much civil engineer as surveyor.

The spring and summer wore away. Though Thoreau was out on his rounds as much as circumstances permitted, he was plainly kept busier than he liked with the graphite business. Late in September he wrote to Blake, "I feel and think rather too much like a business man, having some very irksome affairs to attend to these months and years on account of my family. This is the way I am serving King Admetus, confound him! If it were not for my relations, I would let the wolves prey on his flocks to their bellies' content." He lacked the time for writing, if not for hiking. "It is easy enough to maintain a family, or a state, but it is hard to maintain these children of your brain . . ."

In October John Brown was again in Concord. Thoreau heard him talk at the Town Hall. Brown was on his way to Virginia to lead the raid on Harper's Ferry, but, of course, he let drop no hint of his plans. Soon after, Blake visited Thoreau; they walked to and around Flint's Pond, and Thoreau made a list of all autumn berries to be seen up to the middle of October and after. Next day, the fifteenth, Thoreau set down a plea for town parks—"Each town should have a park, or rather a primitive forest, of five hundred or a thousand acres, where a stick should never be cut for fuel, a common possession forever, for instruction and recreation. . . . All Walden Wood might have been preserved for our park forever, with Walden in its midst, and the Easterbrooks Country, an unoccupied area of some four square miles, might have been our huckleberry-field. . . . A town is an institution which deserves to be remembered."

In Virginia, Brown led eighteen of his men in an attack on Harper's Ferry, hoping to foment a slave insurrection and establish a free state in the Appalachians from which to spread rebellion to the south. The insurrection did not take place, and Brown and those of his followers who survived were taken prisoner by forces under Colonel Robert E. Lee. By the nineteenth of October, word of that abortive stroke against the institution of slavery had reached Concord and so excited Thoreau that he wrote two thousand words about the event in his journal. He looked past all legal questions and saw only that here was a man who had dared at last to strike out against an abhorrent situation. However much Thoreau disliked violence, he was prepared to support violence against an institution about which he felt so strongly.

In subsequent days, he poured more of his thoughts about Brown and slavery into his journal, and by the end of that month he had reassembled these paragraphs into a lecture and announced that he would speak in Concord on behalf of John Brown. He was advised not to, that feeling was against Brown and his rash act. When the selectmen refused to ring the bell of the Town Hall to announce the hour of the lecture, Thoreau did it himself. He delivered his lecture to a partially hostile audience October 30.

Though he outlined Brown's life, his lecture was not so much a plea for Brown, as it was a defense of principle, an urgent plea that civil disobedience be continued, and that, if all else failed, violence in a good cause could be condoned. He spoke forcefully, with deep conviction, and if he did not dispel entirely the hostility of his audience, he abated it. He was particularly vehement about the attitude of the press in its condemnation of John Brown. "The newspapers seem to ignore, or perhaps are

185

really ignorant, of the fact that there are at least as many as two or three individuals to a town throughout the North who think much as the present speaker does about him and his enterprise. I do not hesitate to say that they are an important and growing party. We aspire to be something more than stupid and timid chattels, pretending to read history and our Bibles, but desecrating every house and every day we breathe in. . . . Why do they still dodge the truth? They are so anxious because of a dim consciousness of the fact, which they do not distinctly face, that at least a million of the free inhabitants of the United States would have rejoiced if it had succeeded. They at most only criticise the tactics."

He asserted that his respect for those fellowmen who were content to follow the path of least resistance in a matter involving so basic a principle was not very high. "Such do not know that like the seed is the fruit, and that, in the moral world, when good seed is planted, good fruit is inevitable, and does not depend on our watering and cultivating; that when you plant, or bury, a hero in his field, a crop of heroes is sure to spring up. This is a seed of such force and vitality, that it does not ask our leave to germinate."

He made no attempt to explain away Brown's defiance of law but put himself squarely on the side of John Brown. "I speak for the slave when I say that I prefer the philanthropy of Captain Brown to that philanthropy which neither shoots me nor liberates me. At any rate, I do not think it is quite sane for one to spend his whole life in talking or writing about this matter, unless he is continuously inspired, and I have not done so. A man may have other affairs to tend to. I do not wish to kill nor to be killed, but I can foresee circumstances in which both these things would be by me unavoidable. . . .

"These men, in teaching us how to die, have at the same time taught us how to live. If this man's acts and words do not create a revival, it will be the severest possible satire on the acts and words that do. It is the best news that America has ever heard. It has already quickened the feeble pulse of the North, and infused more and more generous blood into her veins and heart than any number of years of what is called commercial and political prosperity could."

Thoreau's plea for Brown was certainly his most successful and powerful address. It was received by his audience with much sympathy and so much applause that the echoes of it reached into Boston. He was asked to repeat it at Theodore Parker's Boston Temple, where it met with the enthusiastic response of the largest audience Thoreau had ever had. Two days later he gave it in Worcester, again to a responsive audience. The newspapers reported it, somewhat garbled, to be sure, but word of Thoreau's defense of Brown was carried in the nation's press. Even Calvin Greene, in faraway Detroit, heard about his plea and wrote about it.

Yet Thoreau was not an Abolitionist. He belonged to no society, no group, however much they might rally behind him. His was the reaction of a man of principle, not of the spokesman for a group committed to a cause. He was not yet done with John Brown. On the second of December he spoke again at the Town Hall at a memorial service for Brown. On the third he drove one of Brown's men, Francis Merriam, to Acton; Merriam was on his way to Canada, for the government was pressing the search for all Brown's fellow conspirators, and even Sanborn absented himself from Concord for a while.

Merriam was unbalanced. Thoreau noted that he "was betrayed by his eyes, which had a glaring film over them and no serene depth into which you could look." Merriam wanted to go to Emerson's house, and told Thoreau certain things he did not want Sanborn to know. "Said 'I know I am insane,'—and I knew it too." Merriam thought Thoreau might be Emerson, but when he was assured that this was not so, he wanted to leave the conveyance. Thoreau discharged the mission successfully.

Then he went back to his beloved ponds, meadows, rivers and hills. On the last day of that active year he was hiking up the Assabet to the sweet-gale meadow, making notes on seed-heads, catkins, tree sparrows, trees, ice-cutters, and reflecting, "How vain to try to teach youth, or anybody, truths! They can only learn them after their own fashion, and when they are ready. I do not mean by this to condemn our system of education, but to show what it amounts to," and concluding that "A man thinks as well through his legs and arms as his brain."—quite as if the attack on Harper's Ferry and the execution of John Brown had never taken place.

CHAPTER 12

"... I Would Know Better How It Would End"

> *I learned this, at least, by my experiment: that if one advances confidently in the direction of his dreams, and endeavors to live the life which he has imagined, he will meet with a success unexpected in common hours. He will put some things behind, will pass an invisible boundary; new, universal, and more liberal laws will begin to establish themselves around and within him; or the old laws be expanded, and interpreted in his favor in a more liberal sense, and he will live with the license of a higher order of beings. In proportion as he simplifies his life, the laws of the universe will appear less complex, and solitude will not be solitude, nor poverty poverty, nor weakness weakness. If you have built castles in the air, your work need not be lost; that is where they should be. Now put the foundations under them.* —WALDEN

WITH the beginning of 1860, Thoreau was at work on two major projects. One, to which he referred as his *Kalendar of Concord,* was to be something similar to but more intimate than Gilbert White's *Natural History of Selborne.* The other was a study of *The Dispersion of Seeds,* undoubtedly intended to be ultimately part of the larger project, the *Kalendar.*

But his writing time was sadly cut into by the hours he

was forced to give to the graphite business. Nor would he decrease his sauntering time and the compilation of his journal. He was much at Walden that winter, and at Fair Haven, where one January day he watched the snow-fleas. "There are a dozen or twenty to a square rod on the very middle of the pond. When I approach one, it commonly hops away, and if it gets a good spring it hops a foot or more, so that it is lost to me. Though they are scarcely the twentieth of an inch long they make these surprising bounds, or else conceal themselves by entering the snow."

Early in February he delivered a new lecture to the Concord Lyceum. This was *Wild Apples*. When the weather did not permit his hiking, he went into Cambridge and took books from the library. That February he was reading Conrad Gesner's *History of Four-footed Beasts* and reflecting, "We cannot spare the very lively and lifelike descriptions of some of the old naturalists. They sympathize with the creatures which they describe."

In February also, James Redpath wrote to Thoreau for an account of John Brown's Battle of Black Jack, Kansas, about which Brown had told Thoreau on the occasion of his visit to the Thoreaus. Redpath had been an assistant of Brown—but not a participant—in the Harper's Ferry attack. The correspondence thus opened led to publication of *A Plea for Captain John Brown* and Thoreau's memorial comments in an anthology of articles edited by Redpath under the title of *Echoes of Harper's Ferry* later in 1860.

In May he wrote a curious letter to Blake, philosophizing about the state of mankind in the world. "Men & boys are learning all kinds of trades but how to make *men* of themselves. They learn to make houses, but they are not so well housed, they are not so contented in their houses, as the woodchucks in their holes. What is the use of a house if you haven't got a tolerable planet to put it on? If you can not tolerate the planet it is on? Grade the ground first. If a man believes and expects great things of himself it makes no odds where you put him, or what you show him . . . he will be surrounded by grandeur. He's in the condition of a healthy & hungry man, who says to himself—How sweet this crust is!"

Thoreau, at least, was not discontented with his attic room, and the stacks of his first book, which were slowly diminishing in response to the orders which came in to him still from isolated readers of *Walden* in various parts of the country. After the details of the graphite business and his hours of sauntering about Concord, he retired almost every evening to his attic room and wrote until it was time to go to bed.

In July Thoreau saw Hawthorne once more. Hawthorne had been abroad, acting as American consul at Liverpool; now he had returned to Concord. Thoreau wrote his sister Sophia, then visiting in Campton, New Hampshire, that Hawthorne had not altered "except that he was looking pretty brown after his voyage. He is as simple & child-like as ever." Thoreau was much concerned this month with the temperature of the brooks and the ponds around Concord, and filled his journal with details about the "cold brooks" and those filled with warmer water.

That summer he was ready for another excursion. He asked Channing to go with him to Monadnock, and, after some delay, Channing agreed to go. They left Concord on the morning of August fourth and were gone six days. They did not always enjoy fair weather. Thoreau filled his journal with all manner of data about the plants, rocks, streams, only occasionally pausing to admire the view. "Each day, about an hour before sunset, I got sight,

191

as it were accidentally, of an elysium beneath me. The smoky haze of the day, suggesting a furnace-like heat, a trivial dustiness, gave place to a clear transparent enamel, through which houses, woods, farms, and lakes were seen as in a picture indescribably fair and expressly made to be looked at."

In an account of the excursion written to Blake that September, "We went up in the rain—wet through, and found ourselves in a cloud there at mid *pm.* in no situation to look about for the best place for a camp. So I proceeded at once, through the cloud, to that memorable stone 'chunk yard,' in which we made our humble camp once, and there, after putting our packs under a rock, having a good hatchet, I proceeded to build a substantial house, which Channing declared the handsomest he ever saw. (He never camped out before, and was, no doubt, prejudiced in its favor.) This was done about dark, and by that time we were nearly as wet as if we had stood in a hogshead of water. We then built a fire before the door, directly on the site of our little camp of two years ago. Standing before this, and turning round slowly, like meat that is roasting, we were as dry if not drier than ever after a few hours, & so, at last, we 'turned in.' . . .

"We & the *mt.* had a sound season, as the saying is. How glad we were to be wet in order that we might be dried!—how glad we were of the storm which made our house seem like a new home to us! . . . Our next house was more substantial still. One side was rock, good for durability, the floor the same, & the roof which I made would have upheld a horse. I stood on it to do the shingling."

Channing, however, was not as good a camper as Thoreau. He worried a little about "what was the largest beast that might nibble his legs there," and was presently ready to "*de-camp*," a day sooner than Thoreau had counted on. Their camp was well concealed, for "Five hundred persons at least came onto the *mt.* while we were there, but not one found our camp."

Once back in Concord, Thoreau was not inclined to go abroad again that year. He declined an invitation from Ricketson to come to New Bedford. "I have enjoyed very much my visits to you and my rides in your neighborhood, and am sorry that I cannot enjoy such things oftener; but life is short, and there are other things also to be done. I admit that you are more social than I am, and far more attentive to 'the common courtesies of life' but this is partly for the reason that you have fewer or less exacting private pursuits." Ricketson had chided him for not writing. "Not to have written a note for a year," Thoreau replied, "is with me a very menial offence. I think that I do not correspond with any one so often as once in six-months."

Early in September, however, Thoreau spoke in Lowell, Massachusetts, where he walked along the Merrimack River on a suddenly crisp morning, seeing "very large plants of the lanceolate thistle, four feet high and very branching." No word of his lecture is set down in his journal. He wrote instead of "the dew on a fine grass in the meadows, which was almost as white and silvery as frost when the rays of the newly risen sun fell on it," seen from the windows of the train as he rode the next morning from Lowell to Boston on his way home. Next day, back in his pattern, he was summoned by George Melvin to look at a lynx killed on the Carlisle road.

He now had ready—despite his excursions in and away from Concord, and despite the press of the graphite business—part of his *Dispersion of Seeds.* This was *The Succession of Forest Trees,* one of the products of his study of

193

tree rings. He delivered it as a lecture before the Middlesex Agricultural Society, which planned to include it in its "Report" later in the year. Before this, however, it occurred to Thoreau that Horace Greeley, who had frequently asked for something from Thoreau's pen, might be interested in seeing it; so he dispatched it to Greeley for the *Tribune,* where Greeley printed it October sixth.

Early in November, writing to Ricketson, Thoreau mentioned his "out-door harvest this fall," and said it had been "one Canada Lynx, a fierce looking fellow, which, it seems, we have hereabouts; eleven barrels of apples from trees of my own planting; and a large crop of white oak acorns which I did not raise." That autumn's harvest, fatefully, had yet another aspect; on the third of December he went out to Smith's Hill to count the rings in some hickory trees. The day was damp and cold. He lay on the ground, the better to count the rings in a trunk broken from the stump too high for him to see. He caught cold.

On his way home he had an argument with Sam Staples and another Concord man, named Walcott, who declared that John Brown had done wrong. "When I said that I thought he was right, they agreed in asserting that he did wrong because he threw his life away, and that no man had a right to undertake anything which he knew would cost him his life. I inquired if Christ did not foresee that he would be crucified if he preached such doctrines as he did, but they both, though as if it was their only escape, asserted that they did not believe that he did. Upon which a third party threw in, 'You do not think that he had so much foresight as Brown.' Of course, they as good as said that, if Christ *had* foreseen that he would be crucified, he would have 'backed out.' Such are the principles and the logic of the mass of men."

Snow fell next day, and Thoreau was confined to the

house. He was still stirred by his argument with Walcott and Staples of the previous day, added to by an article in the *New York Tribune* about a demand levied upon an escaped slave in Toronto. "Talk about slavery!" he wrote. "It is not the peculiar institution of the South. It exists wherever men are bought and sold, wherever a man allows himself to be made a mere thing or a tool, and surrenders his inalienable rights of reason and conscience. Indeed, this slavery is more complete than that which enslaves the body alone."

Though his cold did not improve, he went to lecture at Waterbury a week later, but on his return he was kept to the house, not alone by his own illness, but also by that of his mother, now confined to her bed. He had to decline an invitation from the curator of the Concord Lyceum to entertain Wendell Phillips when he came to Concord to lecture that month. His mother slowly improved; Thoreau's improvement was slower and not lasting.

For much of that winter he stayed at home. His journal for 1861 opened with paragraphs clearly intended for a lecture—on wild berries ("I think that our various species of berries are our *wild fruits* to be compared with the more celebrated ones of the tropics")—and went on with the contents of a crow's stomach brought to him by the younger Horace Mann, quotations from books under study, notes on the depth of the snow ("two feet deep on a level now"), a screech owl caught in Hastings's barn on the meeting-house avenue, also brought by Mann, reports of Walden brought by Channing—but his entries were no longer daily, and longer hiatuses occurred.

On March 22nd he wrote Ricketson, "To tell the truth, I am not on the alert for the signs of spring, not having had any winter yet. I took a severe cold about the 3 of Dec., which at length resulted in a kind of bronchitis, so that I have been confined to the house ever since, excepting a very few experimental trips as far as the P.O. in some particularly mild noons. My health otherwise has not been affected in the least, nor my spirits. I have simply been imprisoned for so long; & it has not prevented my doing a good deal of reading & the like."

On May 3d he wrote Blake, "I am still as much an invalid as when you & Brown were here, if not more of one, and at this rate there is danger that the cold weather may come again, before I get over my bronchitis. The Doctor accordingly tells me that I must 'clear out,' to the West Indies, or elsewhere, he does not seem to care much where." The Indies were out of the question "on account of their muggy heat in the summer," and the cost of a trip to Europe was beyond him. He thought of going to Minnesota. "The inland air may help me at once, or it may not." He tried to persuade Blake to go along; Blake could not go. He next tried Channing, who was loath to be gone from Concord for so long.

At last he turned to young Horace Mann, who had been supplying him with specimens throughout the winter. Mann was the son of the famous educator of the same name, who had died in August, 1859, after which his family had moved to Concord. Mann accepted his invitation, and on Sunday, May 12, they set out, going by way of Worcester where they paused to visit Blake and Brown and another man—"a dry humorist, a gentlemen who has been a sportsman and was well acquainted with dogs." Thence to Albany and Schenectady, and so westward.

At this point, Thoreau virtually abandoned his journal. He was a sick man, and he was well aware of it. He had now grown a bushy beard, and looked much older than his 44 years. His illness prevented him from appreciating the journey. He could have written an outstanding account of this longest excursion, had he been in good health. One aspect of the passing landscape caught his eye. "I began to notice from the cars a tree with handsome rose-colored flowers. At first I thought it some variety of thorn; but it was not long before the truth flashed on me, that this was my long-sought Crab-Apple." To find this tree had long been an ambition of Thoreau's, yet wherever the train stopped, there seemed to be none.

In Minnesota at last he saw the wild pigeon, he studied the wild gophers, and observed the greater wildness of the country—but he did so as a sick man does, not with the fever of discovery and the compulsion to communicate his discoveries. And at last he found the wild crab-apple —"about eight miles west of St. Anthony's Falls; touched it and smelled it, and secured a lingering corymb of flowers for my herbarium." This discovery alone stood out in his memory and was embodied in his revision of *Wild Apples*.

On June 25 he wrote Sanborn from Redwing, Minnesota, that he had "performed this journey in a very dead and alive manner." The Civil War had begun, but "I am not even so well informed as to the progress of the war as you suppose. . . . The people of Minnesota have *seemed* to me more cold—to feel less implicated in this war, than the people of Massachusetts." He wrote at length of the landscape. "The grand feature hereabouts is, of course, the Mississippi River. Too much can hardly be said of its grandeur, & the beauty of this portion of it. . . . it flows from the pine to the palm."

At last he was close to more Indians than he had ever known before. The Sioux were still very much in Minnesota, and still menacing the white man's way of life, as the New Ulm uprising next year was to prove. But his interest in the Indians had flagged with his health. "After spending some three weeks in and about St. Paul, St. Anthony, and Minneapolis, we made an excursion in a steamer some 300 or more miles up the Minnesota (St. Peter's) River, to Redwood, and the Lower Sioux Agency, in order to see the plains & the Sioux, who were to receive their annual payment there. . . .

"A regular council was held with the Indians, who had come in on their ponies, and speeches were made on both sides thro' an interpreter, quite in the described mode; the Indians, as usual, having the advantage in point of truth and earnestness, and therefore of eloquence. The most prominent chief was named Little Crow. They were quite dissatisfied with the white man's treatment of them & probably have reason to be so. . . .

"In the afternoon the half naked Indians performed a dance, at the request of the Governor, for our amusement & their own benefit & then we took leave of them & of the officials who had come to treat with them."

But Thoreau was now ready for home. "Our faces are set toward home. Will you please let my sister know that we shall *probably* start for Milwaukee & Mackinaw in a day or 2 . . . *via Prairie du Chien* & not La Crosse."

Home again, Thoreau thought himself in somewhat better health. He wrote Ricketson in August that he was "considerably, yet not essentially better, my cough still continuing." He added that he might be obliged "to go to another climate again very soon," and complained that his "ordinary pursuits, both indoor and out, have been for the most part omitted, or seriously interrupted—walking, boating, scribbling, &c. Indeed, I have been sick so long that I have almost forgotten what it is to be well, yet I feel that it all respects only my envelope." Two months later, in mid-October, he wrote Ricketson that he

198

had been riding about in a wagon owned by Edward Hoar, "every other day." But his letter was short. "It is easy to talk, but hard to write."

By the beginning of 1862, it was evident to Thoreau that he was not improving, and that in all probability he would not get better. As so often happens to literary men, at this point in his life, when it was all but over, there was a rising tide of appreciation of his work. Myron Benton wrote him from Dutchess County, New York, "I read and re-read your books with ever fresh delight. Nor is it pleasure alone; there is a singular spiritual healthiness with which they seem imbued,—the expression of a soul essentially sound, so free from any morbid tendency." Thoreau replied two months later to say, "if I were to live, I should have much to report on Natural History generally. You ask particularly after my health. I *suppose* that I have not many months to live; but, of course, I know nothing about it. I may add that I am enjoying existence as much as ever, and regret nothing."

Theophilus Brown wrote that "The demand for your books here seems to be rather on the increase," and ordered two copies of *A Week on the Concord and Merrimack Rivers,* of which Thoreau had by this time disposed of slightly over a hundred copies. At the same time, Ticknor & Fields, Thoreau's publishers, proposed bringing out his first book again—which meant binding the unbound sheets Thoreau took over from Munroe—and bringing out a second edition of *Walden,* from which Thoreau indicated that he wanted the subtitle, *Life in the Woods,* deleted.

Ticknor & Fields had also, in late 1859, taken over *The Atlantic Monthly.* The new editor was James T. Fields, who wrote Thoreau for contributions to the magazine. Thoreau replied in February, making clear that he "should expect no sentiment or sentence be altered or omitted without my consent." He sent in *Autumnal Tints* and, a few days later, *The Higher Law,* which, at Fields's suggestion, he retitled *Life without Principle.* Then he got to work at revision of *Walking, Wild Apples, Night and Moonlight.*

He was dying, and knew it, of tuberculosis. But next to sauntering through the countryside he loved, he must have enjoyed, as far as was possible, lingering over the sentences and paragraphs he had written in healthier days. "I wish to speak a word for Nature, for absolute freedom and wildness, as contrasted with a freedom and culture merely civil,—to regard man as an inhabitant, or a part and parcel of Nature, rather than a member of society. . . . the walking of which I speak . . . is itself the enterprise and adventure of the day. . . . I believe in the forest, and in the meadow, and in the night in which the corn grows."

One cannot doubt that he walked his beloved lanes and byways in spirit in these months, and lived again those afternoons and nights in Nature. "Night is . . . less profane than day. . . . It must be allowed that the light of the moon, sufficient though it is for the pensive walker, and not disproportionate to the inner light we have, is very inferior in quality and intensity to that of the sun. But the moon is not to be judged alone by the quantity of light she sends to us, but also by her influence on the earth and its inhabitants. . . . I speak out of the night. . . . the beauty of moonlight is seen over lonely pastures where cattle are silently feeding. . . . Every plant and field and forest emits its odor now, swamp-pink in the meadow and tansy in the road . . . We hear the tinkling of rills which we never detected before. . . . The stars are the jewels of the night, . . . a man could get along with *them,*—though he was considerably reduced in his circumstances,— . . . a kind of bread and cheese that never failed. . . . Great restorer of antiquity, great enchanter. . . . New and old things are confounded. . . . Consider the moonlight, so civil, yet so savage!"

As he weakened, his sister Sophia took letters at his dictation, and helped with the revision of his essays, all destined for *The Atlantic Monthly.* His friends came to call, even to Sam Staples, his onetime jailer, who had since on occasion served as Thoreau's rodman when he surveyed the town. He told Emerson later that he had never spent an hour with more satisfaction; "Never saw a man dying with so much pleasure and peace." His Aunt Louisa asked Thoreau whether he had made his peace with God; Thoreau replied, "I never knew that we had quarrelled." Channing mourned his approaching solitude; Thoreau told him, "It is better some things should end."

Another visitor strove to comfort Thoreau by pointing out that death was the common lot of all people. Thoreau replied, "When I was a boy, I learned that I must die, so I am not disappointed now; death is as near to you as it is to me." He fretted a little because the children did not come oftener to see him. "I love them as if they were my own," he said. And to another well-meaning visitor who sought to talk to him about the next world, he said only, "One world at a time."

On the morning of May sixth, a fine, sunny morning, just after a neighbor had brought him some hyacinths, he sank back on his couch, closed his eyes, murmured "moose" and "Indian," and slept quietly away in his forty-fifth year.

He was buried from the parish church at a public funeral at which Emerson spoke. He said of Thoreau that "No truer American existed" and praised his "wonderful fitness of body and mind. He could pace sixteen rods more accurately than another man could measure them with rod and chain. He could find his path in the woods at night, he said, better by his feet than his eyes. He could estimate the measure of a tree very well by his eyes; he could estimate the weight of a calf or a pig, like a dealer. From a box containing a bushel or more of loose pencils, he could take up with his hands fast enough just a dozen pencils at every grasp. He was a good swimmer, runner, skater, boatman, and would probably outwalk most countrymen in a day's journey. And the relation of body to mind was still finer than we have indicated."

He praised his "robust common sense, armed with stout hands, keen perceptions, and strong will" as well as his "excellent wisdom." And, prophetically, he concluded with, "The country knows not yet, or in the least part, how great a son it has lost. It seems an injury that he should leave in the midst his broken task, which none else can finish,—a kind of indignity to so noble a soul, that he should depart out of Nature before yet he has been really shown to his peers for what he is. But he, at least, is content. His soul was made for the noblest society; he had in a short life exhausted the capabilities of this world; wherever there is knowledge, wherever there is virtue, wherever there is beauty, he will find a home."

After this long eulogy, Thoreau was carried to his grave in the New Burying Ground, at the foot of Bedford Street, though some years later his remains were removed to the Sleepy Hollow Cemetery. Concord had lost its most distinguished son, and the nation a man and writer unique in any age.

Afterword

> *One of the great names in American literature is the name of Henry Thoreau. Yet only after sixty years is he slowly coming into his own.*
>
> —VERNON L. PARRINGTON
> *Main Currents in American Thought*

THOREAU'S fame was slow to grow, his influence slow to spread. Yet neither spread as fast as that very materialism he so scorned. Emerson's eulogy was published in the August 1862 issue of *The Atlantic Monthly,* and various other tributes found their way into print. The essays Thoreau had revised in the months of his long dying came rapidly into print in *The Atlantic Monthly,* and Ticknor & Fields reprinted *Walden* in 1863, 1864, and 1866; even *A Week on the Concord and Merrimack Rivers* was reprinted in 1862 and again in 1868. In 1863 the same publishers brought out the essays collected under the title of *Excursions,* in 1864 *The Maine Woods,* and in 1865 both *Cape Cod* and Emerson's selection of Thoreau's letters. These books found a waiting and slowly growing audience, despite a somewhat deprecatory view of Thoreau as an eccentric written by James Russell Lowell and published in *The North American Review.*

In 1873 Ellery Channing's biography of Thoreau—*Thoreau, the Poet-Naturalist,*—appeared; but this, which was more Channing than Thoreau, added nothing to his then small fame. Sanborn's biography came in 1882; it was scarcely more satisfying. It took an Englishman, H. S. Salt, to write a balanced life of Thoreau in 1890, and a Frenchman, Léon Bazalgette, in *Henry Thoreau. Sauvage* (1924), to point out that Thoreau's significance was greater than his age had suspected.

Thoreau's influence, by the turn of the century, was instanced by more than one world leader, and in various parts of the world. Count Leo Tolstoi wrote in 1901 of it in *A Message to the American People*—published, ironically, in that very same magazine which had given space to Lowell's deprecation of Thoreau. The British Labor Party, which grew out of the theories of Karl Marx and William Morris, urged members to buy and carry with them a pocket edition of *Walden,* as best embodying their essential philosophy. And the Mahatma Gandhi took from Thoreau's *Civil Disobedience* the philosophy of passive resistance which led to India's freedom, while countless numbers of writers—William Butler Yeats, W. H. Hudson, H. M. Tomlinson, many another—testified to the importance of Thoreau in their lives. His native country has only recently recognized Thoreau's significance to the extent of including *Walden* among less than a score of essential classics of democracy and distributed throughout the world in many languages by the United States Information Agency.

Today, a century after his death, the name of Henry D. Thoreau appears on every list of that small handful of American writers considered to be the greatest.

Bibliographical Notes

THE reader who wishes to read Thoreau or to learn more about him and his work will find, as I did, certain books indispensable. Foremost among them is *The Writings of Henry David Thoreau* (Walden Edition, in 20 volumes: Houghton Mifflin Company, 1906). The student ought to avoid the four volumes of the *Journal* edited by Harrison Blake, because of the unhappily arbitrary arrangement of the entries, which destroys the continuity of the *Journal*. Next to the Walden Edition of Thoreau stands *The Correspondence of Henry David Thoreau*, edited by Walter Harding and Carl Bode (New York University Press, 1958). These are the basic sources necessary to any knowledge of the writings of Thoreau. In addition, the reader will want *A Thoreau Handbook*, by Walter Harding (New York University Press, 1959), the best available guide through Thoreau scholarship.

The early biographies of Thoreau are all interesting —*Thoreau, the Poet Naturalist*, by William Ellery Channing (Roberts, 1873); *Henry D. Thoreau*, by F. B. Sanborn (Houghton Mifflin Company, 1882); *The Life of Henry David Thoreau*, by Henry S. Salt (Richard Bentley & Son, London, 1890—the best of the biographies before 1900)—but perhaps the most complete, despite several moot points in the text, is *Thoreau*, by Henry Seidel

Canby (Houghton Mifflin Company, 1939). Also of value to the student interested in Thoreau's background is *Concord: American Town,* by Townsend Scudder (Little, Brown and Company, 1947).

The student who wishes merely to sample Thoreau will find four very fine samplers available. First among them is *The Portable Thoreau,* edited by Carl Bode (The Viking Press, 1947); this has no peer. Three books which are cross-sections of the *Journal* seemed to me especially effective in conveying the flavor of that remarkable work; these are *The Heart of Thoreau's Journals,* edited by Odell Shepard (Houghton Mifflin Company, 1927), *Men of Concord,* edited by F. H. Allen (Houghton Mifflin Company, 1936), and *H. D. Thoreau: A Writer's Journal,* edited by Laurence Stapleton (Dover Publications, 1962).

Finally, that scholar who wishes to delve more deeply into Thoreau's relation to his world will find two books of especial importance—*Henry David Thoreau,* by Joseph Wood Krutch (William Sloane Associates, 1948), and *The Shores of America: Thoreau's Inward Exploration,* by Sherman Paul (The University of Illinois Press, 1958).

AUGUST DERLETH

Sauk City, Wisconsin

Index

209

211

212

A̲UGUST DERLETH

began writing in 1922 at the age of thirteen. Since then many short stories, essays, reviews, poems, novels and other books have appeared under the August Derleth byline or one of his pen names. His most widely popular novels have been *Wind Over Wisconsin, The Shield of the Valiant* and *Bright Journey*. His Sac Prairie Saga was projected as a group of approximately fifty books designed to portray the social and economic life and history of a typical Wisconsin village from about 1830 to 1950. Many of these books have already been published. Mr. Derleth has spent practically all his life in Sauk City, Wisconsin, where he was born and where he still makes his home.